THERE'S ROOM AT THE TOP

"In *There's Room at the Top*, Matthew and George Rekers have successfully collaborated to produce a concise and challenging format to encourage all of us who seek excellence in our lives, both professionally and personally."

"I recommend it as required reading for everyone aspiring and committed to taking the steps necessary to reach 'The Top.' The reader will not be disappointed in what the Rekers have to offer."

—James A. Dismore
Chairman and CEO, Ultimate Support Systems, Inc.
Former Vice President, Wal-Mart

"In *There's Room at the Top,* Matthew and George Rekers offer a strategic and disciplined process for the diagnosis and treatment of organizational and leadership weaknesses and deficiencies. The serious reader is likely to be inspired as well as enlightened to the potential in themselves and their organization. I highly recommend this book for the individual aspiring to improve their own managerial performance and the performance of their organization."

—Professor Debra Beazley, Ph.D., M.B.A.
Director of Business Studies, Troy State University
Former corporate executive

"There's Room at the Top offers profound and meaningful insight into how spiritual principles can transform leadership at every level. The challenges that organizations face are real, as are the truths in this book. Dr. Rekers and his son, Matthew, have developed a process that is easy to digest, but profound in its implications."

—Michael R. Brenan
President, BB&T of South Carolina

THERE'S ROOM AT THE TOP

33 Dynamics for Managerial Excellence

How you can lead your company to
world-class performance

MATTHEW G. REKERS, M.B.A.
GEORGE A. REKERS, Ph.D., M.B.A.

UXBRIDGE PUBLISHING LTD. CO.

Published by Uxbridge Publishing Ltd. Co.,
Minden, Nevada, a subsidiary of
Phurneaux Llfracombe Strazzeleski Ltd.

33Dynamics books may be purchased for educational, business, or sales promotional use. For information please write:
33Dynamics LLC, P.O. Box 346, Columbia, SC 29202.
www.33dynamics.com

ISBN 0-9749990-0-8

Edited by David Kremenak

Printed in the United States of America

10 9 8 7 6 5 4 3 2 1

This book is dedicated to helping executives, business owners, managers, and entrepreneurs take their companies to ever higher levels of excellence.

Contents

Acknowledgments

Without the significant influence of others on our thinking, this book would not exist.

We would like to thank Jörg Knoblauch, Ph.D., M.B.A., who gave us a personal tour of Drilbox, the Knoblauch Group Company that received the acclaimed business award as the most efficient company from the German government. We were inspired to write this book by our first-hand observations of this world-class model of executive management and organizational effectiveness.

We are particularly indebted to several astute readers who invested many hours reading drafts of the manuscript and giving us their frank feedback. For their insights, we would like to thank professor Debra Beazley, Ph.D., M.B.A., Mike Bledsoe, Mike Brenan, James Dismore, Daniel Graves, M.Div., Darshan Jayashekar, M.S., David Kremenak, Jonathan Lomas, James McCune, Rick Milne, M.D., Jay Pitts, Steven Rekers, C.P.A., M.B.A., Andrew Rekers, Timothy Rekers, Mark Rekers, professor Ed Sherbert, D.B.A., M.B.A., and Lew Wayburn.

We also acknowledge insights gained through extensive group discussions with Randall Cooper, M.B.A., Ricki Cox, M.B.A., and Debbie Walker, M.B.A. We also thank professor Ron Snyder, D.B.A., M.B.A., a former corporate executive and management consultant, for his expert advice and for providing us with some very helpful resources. Finally, we are deeply thankful to our family and friends for their love and support.

Preface

Leading for Maximum Performance

"The last two decades have been a period of wrenching change for many businesses and their employees. Many managers have learned that cherished ways of doing business do not work anymore and that major changes must be made in the way organizations are managed and work gets done. These changes are so great that some observers view them as a second industrial revolution."

—Professors Jeannie M. Folk,
Ray H. Garrison & Eric W. Noreen[1]

The authors of a popular M.B.A. textbook made this astute comment. We agree. Companies need to change their ineffective ways of conducting business, or they'll find themselves out of business—fast!

In this environment of massive continuous change, what empowers highly successful executives to take their company to the top? Executive power flows from specific knowledge and specific management skills. Highly effective executives know how to sharpen their company's competitive edge in today's rapidly shifting market. And how do they do that? They skillfully lead their organizations through necessary transformations that maximize their ability to serve and please customers.

Adroitly adjusting to rapid change, the best executives actively implement improvement programs such as just-in-time (JIT), total quality management (TQM), six sigma, and process reengineering—to name a few. Through such action, they boldly reduce costs, increase quality, increase output, increase delivery performance, earn customer "fans," and thereby maximize profits for shareholders.[2]

So that's the big picture. But any manager worth his or her salt immediately asks, "*Specifically speaking*, exactly how do successful executives maximize their company's performance?" Alert managers at every level are well aware of the very common challenges that create a drag on a company's overall performance:

- Customer attrition causing loss of market share
- Ineffective employees
- Bottlenecks in processes
- Inadequate marketing
- Excessively large inventories
- Product quality problems
- Service quality problems
- Excessive employee turnover
- Delivery problems
- Supply problems
- Difficulties with suppliers
- A disorganized workplace
- Information overload or lack of pertinent data
- Team problems
- Work inefficiencies
- Control problems
- Challenging ethical dilemmas
- Slow product turnover

- Unbalanced lifestyles of managers
- Unmotivated employees
- Stress-induced employee absence, illness, or lowered performance
- Disgruntled employees
- Disgruntled customers
- Communication problems
- Lack of clearly articulated company goals
- Cash flow problems
- Shrinkage due to both employee and customer theft
- Unqualified workers
- Poor public relations
- Inadequate strategic planning

These problems, and more, confront managers in today's marketplace. All these challenges must be fully conquered to maximize company performance. Sound down right impossible? Well, the top executives today manage to continually succeed in mastering these very challenges.

Business professors, best selling authors, and some of these stellar executives themselves write books to describe how such top performance is achieved. But, realistically speaking, in the daily pressures of managing your company, you cannot be expected to be able to read dozens of such books to carefully "mine" them for all the pearls of wisdom you need to achieve managerial excellence yourself. You cannot devote weeks and months to library research, interviewing successful executives, pursuing advanced business degrees, and frequently visiting your local bookstore to pursue the latest helpful source of management knowledge.

So we expect that you'll be pleased to know that we have already carefully searched and found the outstanding management practices used by leading companies today. We laboriously combed through the best management textbooks and popular business best sellers for you. We did this to identify the most practical management ideas and specific action plans that highly successful executives use. So we've done the "homework" for you. This book and its related seminar and consulting services provide a summary of the best practical executive practices currently available from such sources as these:

- ❖ *Good to Great: Why Some Companies Make the Leap... and Others Don't* by Jim Collins
- ❖ *In Search of Excellence: Lessons from America's Best-Run Companies* by Thomas J. Peters & Robert H. Waterman, Jr.
- ❖ *The E Myth Revisited: Why Most Small Businesses Don't Work and What to Do About It* by Michael E. Gerber
- ❖ *What Really Works: The 4+2 Formula For Sustained Business Success* by Joyce William, Nohria Nitin, & Bruce Roberson
- ❖ *The One Minute Manager* by Kenneth Blanchard & Spencer Johnson
- ❖ *The McKinsey Way: Using the Techniques of the World's Top Strategic Consultants to Help You and Your Business* by Ethan Rasiel
- ❖ *Out of the Crisis* by Edward W. Deming
- ❖ *The Human Side of Enterprise* by Douglas McGregor
- ❖ *Managerial Excellence: McKinsey Award Winners from the Harvard Business Review 1980-1994* by Gupta Rajat
- ❖ *Business Process Benchmarking: Finding and Implementing Best Practices* by Robert Camp
- ❖ *Benchmarking For Best Practices* by Christopher E. Bogan & Michael J. English
- ❖ *Best Practices: Building Your Business with Customer-Focused Solutions* by Robert Hiebeler, Thomas Kelly & Charles Ketteman
- ❖ *The Six Sigma Way: How GE, Motorola, and Other Top Companies Are Honing Their Performance* by Peter S. Pande, Robert P. Neuman & Roland R. Cavanagh
- ❖ *Built to Last: Successful Habits of Visionary Companies* by James C. Collins & Jerry I. Porras
- ❖ *Beyond Integrity* by Scott B. Rae & Kenman L. Wong
- ❖ *Reflections on Leadership: How Robert K. Greenleaf's Theory of Servant-Leadership Influenced Today's Top Management Thinkers* edited by Larry C. Spears

- ❖*Executive Coaching: Practices and Perspectives* by Catherine Fitzgerald & Jennifer Garvey Berger
- ❖*Management* by Thomas S. Bateman & Scott A. Snell
- ❖*Marketing Management* by Philip Kotler
- ❖*Behavior in Organizations* by Jerald Greenberg & Robert A. Baron
- ❖*Introduction to Managerial Accounting* by Jeannie M. Folk, Ray H. Garrison & Eric W. Noreen
- ❖*Retailing Management* by Michael Levy & Barton A. Weitz
- ❖ *Operations Management for Competitive Advantage, Ninth Edition* by Richard B. Chase, Nicholas J. Aquilano & F. Robert Jacobs
- ❖ *The Manager's Bookshelf* by Jon L. Pierce & John W. Newstrom
- ❖ *Moral Issues in Business* by William H. Shaw & Vincent Barry
- ❖*Handbook of Public Relations, Sixth Edition* by Von Essen, Skinner,Von Essen & Mersham
- ❖ *Key Management Ratios: How to Analyse, Compare and Control the Figures that Drive Company Value* by Ciaran Walsh
- ❖*Business Research Methods, Seventh Edition* by William G. Zikmund
- ❖*International Management* by Richard M. Hodgetts & Fred Luthans
- ❖*Strategic Management: Formulation, Implementation, and Control, Eighth Edition* by John A. Pierce II & Richard B. Robinson Jr.

We've culled through all these books and many other leading sources to gather what every executive needs to reach the top. This book—with its associated resources at www.33dynamics.com—is your one-stop resource for the best, practical management approaches to sharpen your company's competitive edge.

Every excellent manager, every top executive, and every alert business owner seeks to maximize company performance. Laurence Holt, a management consultant and Senior Research Fellow at the University of Reading in the United Kingdom, captured the executive's task powerfully:

> "The servant leader is there to facilitate, to empower and release the effectiveness of those working with him. In that sense, he or she is underneath all the other workers in the organization, enabling them to perform."[3]

The best executives unleash the full potential of their company by leading in a way that releases the greatest effectiveness of his or her organization and its employees.

The power of servant leadership to tap the most from one's employees can certainly produce the highest level of service to customers—service that is way beyond their expectations. When you "wow" your customers, they become your enthusiastic fans. And, as we all know, maximum profits can only come from thoroughly pleasing your customers.

So please enjoy! Consider how you can customize your own executive action plans after taking a close look at the best practices of exemplary executives who took their companies all the way to the top. Why not join them? There's still plenty of room at the top!

—George Rekers, Ph.D., M.B.A.
Matthew Rekers, M.B.A.
January 1, 2004 at Interlaken, Switzerland

INTRODUCTION

DISCOVER THE STEPS TO THE TOP

"From where I stand, the elevator to the top is, has been, and always will be 'out of order.' In order to get to the top, you'll have to take the stairs—and you'll have to take them one at a time."

—JOHN HAMMOND, sales executive[1]

Many business executives proudly assert, "We cannot be compared with other businesses." But consider our friendly warning: Do not make such a statement too fast! Why? Because so many leading companies actually improve their performance by comparing their management practices to that of high performing companies.

From the very beginning, Sam Walton looked at other companies so he could implement the very best practices in his own business. This is what he had to say about it:

> "The discount idea was the future. We had only two choices: stay in the variety store business and be hit hard by the discounting wave, or open a discount store. So I started running all over the country, studying the concept, from the mill stores in the East to California, where Sol Price had started his Fed-Mart in 1955. I liked Sol's Fed-Mart name, so I latched right on to Wal-Mart. On July 2, 1962, we opened Wal-Mart No. 1 in Roger, Arkansas, right down the road from Bentonville. We did a million dollars in a year."[2]

One secret to Wal-Mart's phenomenal success is that Sam Walton practiced a form of "benchmarking." He aggressively matched the current best practices of other successful retailers. Then he pushed even farther to exceed the best, setting new benchmarks so high that he left his competition behind in the dust. Even today, competitors struggle to catch up with Wal-Mart's strategic placement of stores and its highly sophisticated real time inventory tracking and vender resupply system.

Because benchmarking is so powerful, highly dedicated executives aggressively seek answers to several pivotal and highly practical questions:

> Question #1—"What, precisely, is benchmarking?"
>
> Question #2—"What set of specific benchmark standards propel companies to the top?"
>
> Question #3—"What are the specific managerial action steps that successful managers have taken to reach those benchmark levels?"

This book directly answers Questions #1 and #2, and this book's associated resources at www.33dynamics.com are offered to executives to answer Question #3.

After gaining a clear concept of benchmarking and its tremendous benefits, the astute executive digs deeper. He or she wants to discover specific practical descriptions of benchmark standards in the full set of management functions that are vital to maximizing company performance.

Many books and articles will discuss a benchmark for a single management function, or benchmarks for just a few functions. But let's be practical! Executive managers need to discover a comprehensive set of benchmarks for a wide range of vital business functions required for top performance. Because this is not available elsewhere, we created this book to fill this gap.

Digging even deeper still, the competent executive—like Sam Walton—wants to investigate the action steps taken by highly effective managers who reach or set the highest current benchmark standards. They learn from the specific successful managerial steps taken by other top performing executives because they want to adapt that practical knowledge to their own company's situation.

Our company's M.B.A. and Ph.D. consultants at 33Dynamics LLC devoted several years of research collecting over 500 specific action steps that top executives have employed to reach benchmark levels in 33 dynamic areas of management of top performing companies. Throughout this book, we offer examples of managerial actions that have been taken to achieve progress toward each benchmark covered. This book's concluding Epilogue discusses how you can easily access all 500+ of these executive action steps so you won't have to reinvent the wheel.

Is Benchmarking New?

Actually, the early Egyptians invented benchmarks. In a recent Tempus business seminar, Dr. Jörg Knoblauch, CEO of the Knoblauch Group Companies in Germany, explained the history of "benchmark" this way (translated from the German): "On a rock, a mark had been hewn in at a definite point to serve as the bench for a stadia rod."[3]

Well, that was about as clear as mud for us. Something was lost in the translation. So we looked up the definition of a "stadia rod" in *Webster's Third New International Dictionary*.[4] Here's how it carefully defines "stadia rod":

> A graduated rod used with an instrument having stadia hairs to measure the distance from the observation point to the place where the rod is positioned by observation of the length of rod subtended by the distance between the stadia hairs when these are fixed or of the space between the stadia hairs when they are adjusted to cover a certain definite interval on the rod.

Wow! Now, doesn't that make it crystal clear where the concept of "benchmarking" came from.

Well, that didn't help us a bit. Perhaps you are a linguistic genius who can understand this kind of "dictionary talk," but the fog factor was way too much for us. So in a desperate attempt to understand ancient Egyptian benchmarking, we made one more try looking up Webster's definition of "benchmark":

> a point of reference from which measurements of any sort may be made.[5]

Now, that's much clearer! In his book, *Business Process Benchmarking*, Robert Camp describes benchmarking as "finding and implementing best practices."[6]

Top business managers today aggressively look for the best business practices found anyplace in the world. These best practices serve as their point of reference for adjusting their own practices to stay competitive in the global marketplace.

Rapid technological advances and fierce competition drive the global economy. These forces can challenge your company's very survival. In this environment of continual change, there are four sources of competitive advantage necessary for your company to survive and to thrive. These "bottom line" practices are

- ❖superior *quality,*
- ❖competitive *cost,*
- ❖effective *innovation*, and
- ❖delivery *speed.*[7]

How can you maintain competitive advantage in these four business functions? By benchmarking. And by doing it before your competitor does.

Of course, benchmarking in business is not brand new. We've already described how Sam Walton used benchmarking in the early 1960's to launch the first of hundreds of extremely successful Wal-Mart retail stores. Xerox was using a benchmarking method in 1979. But even before that, companies in Japan introduced a form of benchmarking.

One Japanese company loaned their employees to another company for a short period of time. By rotating their employees to similar jobs in another business, the workers mastered different processes and brought new ideas back to their home company. Similarly, the German airline Lufthansa arranged for its employees to supervise the work of other airlines all over the world. This corporate practice elevated Lufthansa to the top because their loaned employees discovered all kinds of improved practices that they brought back to their regular work assignments.[8]

What, Then, is New?

Benchmarking practices proved highly profitable for these and other global giants. But notice this practical reality. Sam Walton traveled "all over the country." He expended much effort to discover the best retailing practices. That Japanese company and Lufthansa had to incur the substantial expense of loaning their employees to the other companies. An executive of a Fortune 500 corporation can invest many millions of dollars in such research and development. Discovering benchmarks can be very costly.

But the executives of small- and many medium-sized businesses may not have the time, expertise, or resources to aggressively track down benchmarks for all their company's various business functions.

Benchmarking in business is not new. But what *is* new is a practical service that delivers a comprehensive set of benchmarked practices together with specific action steps that other firms have taken to move up to those benchmark levels.

How You Can Benchmark to Reach the Top

Instead of searching around the globe for benchmarks and loaning your employees to the best companies to learn the action steps necessary to implement those benchmarks, 33Dynamics LLC offers to deliver these benefits to small- and medium-sized companies. How? We offer these benefits through our management books, seminars, executive coaching, and consulting services.

> *"Good ideas most often flow from the process of taking a hard look at your customers, your competitors, and your business all at once."*[9]

THERE'S ROOM AT THE TOP

PROLOGUE

GO FOR THE GOLD

"It is only by finding better practices through benchmarking and incorporating them in the work processes that the desired results will be achieved."
—ROBERT C. CAMP, *Business Process Benchmarking*[1]

Are You Merely Playing "Survivor"? Or Are You Out to Perform at the Olympic Medal Level?

Suppose you have just been hired as a new CEO to turn around a company that is barely hanging on, merely surviving in its industry. Without significant new executive leadership, there is the possibility that your company may not survive at all in the not too distant future. How can you position your company to perform at a world-class Bronze Medal Level, Silver Medal Level, or even the Gold Medal Level of performance—achieving market dominance in your industry and producing all-time record profits?

Say you've identified the highest level of performance—the benchmark—for a particular business function that is vital to your company. When you compare your company's performance in that area, you might be doing very well—functioning just a little short of the benchmark level. In that case, it may not take many managerial steps to match or even surpass the benchmark level, putting you substantially ahead of your competition.

But in other cases, it is not at all unusual to discover that compared to companies performing at the benchmark level for a particular business function, your company is barely surviving. You're not just a little short of the benchmark level. Instead, your company falls far short of the best practice in that business function. In this case, you will need to take a larger number of managerial steps to reach the "best practices" level.

We at 33Dynamics LLC, identified 33 dynamic areas of company performance that are crucial for the success of small- and medium-sized companies. Then we identified seven levels of functioning for each of these 33 dynamic areas:

1. **"Endangered Survivor Level":** For any of the 33 areas of company functioning a company totally lacks all features of the benchmark practice. The very survival of that company is threatened by this fact because its competitors are functioning at a higher level. The company is very close to going out of business.

2. **"Struggling Survivor Level":** A company is not on the verge of closing, but its performance in a given area is so weak that its managers must struggle just to keep their head above water every month. While this is one step on the way toward the benchmark level, it falls far short of the best practice.

3. **"Enduring Survivor Level":** A company is plugging along at 25 miles-per-hour in a 55 miles-per-hour zone, so as to speak. The company is moving forward with a modicum of effectiveness that has worked for awhile, but those with more high-powered engines are speeding ahead of this firm every day. In the short run, the company gets by, but the long-term prospects do not look bright unless more of the features of benchmark levels of performance can be put into practice. It is as if you are in an Olympic trial and you are not coming in last among the bunch of competitors. But at this rate, you have no chance of winning a medal.

4. **"Bronze Medal Level":** This company is well on its way to achieving the best practice level for a business function. It has already implemented some strategic action steps that are taking it to an ever higher level of performance in this business function. The firm may still have a considerable distance to go to match the benchmark, but it is way ahead of many other companies in this regard.

5. "**Silver Medal Level**": A company is functioning just a little shy of implementing the highest benchmark level of performance. It has only a few more steps to take before it will be able to cross the finish line tied for first place.

6. "**Gold Medal Level**": You are a big winner! You have crossed the finish line tied for first place, having fully matched the benchmark level of performance for a business function that is vital for your competitive advantage. You may have tied for "first place" along side your fiercest competitor. Or, you may be way ahead of your nearest competitor because you just "tied for first place" with a company in a different industry that established that benchmark.

There is only one step higher than "tying for first place," and that is to be the *only* "number one" in a competition. You might lead your employees to devise a technology or business practice that goes significantly beyond the existing benchmark level. That would place you at the very top—"number one" with no equal.

Admittedly, this level is highly unusual to achieve. But imagine this: For a specific function that is vital for business, you can aspire to actually *set the new benchmark* level for all industries around the globe! Why not? Why not aspire to outdo the very best in the world? Why not race ahead to be the global leader at the cutting edge of human progress? Sometimes it does not take a huge research and development budget to do so. Sometimes, it does not take a business degree to create a business solution that can benefit business around the world. Consider college drop-out Bill Gates and his invention of computer software used by companies around the globe. Some innovations have cost nothing more than the executive's time to think carefully about how a business function might be accomplished more effectively and/or more efficiently.

You can be a resounding success by just moving your company step by step to the benchmark "Gold Medal" levels in all of the 33 dynamic areas of company performance that we have identified. But we have reserved the term "**Platinum Level**" for those who discover or innovate a new, higher level of performance that exceeds the existing benchmark set by other top global companies. There truly is room at the top, and once you've arrived there, there's even room to kick the top up another notch or two.

The *very best* must be your standard in all areas of company performance if you want to achieve and sustain a competitive advantage. If your competitors have not reached the benchmark level for a specific area of management, but you've led your company to that best practice, then you definitely have a powerful advantage over your competitor in that area.

But if your competitor already raced ahead of you to attain a benchmark level in some management function, then your company risks losing market share to that competitor unless you can catch up.

So you must continually lead your company to work toward the best practices in all areas of your management if you want to survive and excel in your business. To attain market dominance, you need to race ahead to lead your company to attain or even exceed benchmark levels before your competitors are able to do so.

Look Outside Your Own Industry

One way to stay ahead of your competitors is to look outside your own industry to get ideas on how to improve performance in your company. State-of-the-art benchmarking is not restricted to one's own industry. Great competitive advantage can be gained by examining parallel business practices in unrelated industries. This is the way to discover practices that propel you to the top with competitive advantage. Here are some examples:

- ❖One of the top corporations in the world, General Electric (GE) "relentlessly benchmarks competitors and companies in other industries."[2]
- ❖A coal-mining company visited Disney World in Orlando, Florida, to discover and copy the technology that Disney uses to maintain the pneumatic process that operates their animation figures.
- ❖Southwest Airlines in the United States studied how the box stop works at the Formula One race. The airline learned components of a more efficient process to completely unload, clean, and reload planes to get them ready for a new flight.
- ❖Food wholesalers, grocery stores, and restaurants can learn

from all other businesses that handle perishable goods and need rapid product turnover.

- ❖ Pharmacies can learn from other high performing businesses that order many products daily.
- ❖ Banks and credit unions can learn from other companies that handle extensive data processing effectively.[3]

Many managers lack a working knowledge of the most effective executive leadership principles. This was true for a new king who had ascended to his deceased father's throne in Israel about two-and-one-half thousand years ago. Ancient Jewish writings tell of the night when God appeared to King Solomon and offered him a wish, "Ask for whatever you want me to give you." How would you have responded to such a fabulous offer? At first glance, Solomon's reply is shocking. Instead of asking for immense wealth, superhuman power, an invincible army, or lasting peace, he replied, "Give me wisdom and knowledge, that I may *lead* this people, for who is able to govern this great people of yours?"[4]

Because King Solomon sought the *wisdom* and *knowledge* necessary for *leadership*, he ended up at the very top, gaining incredible wealth, riches, knowledge, insight, political dominance, and honor such as no king before him had ever enjoyed.

We suspect that you do not intend to be the usual breed of manager. Like Solomon, you too can seek wisdom and knowledge to lead your company. You can take the strategic steps to master the 33 managerial dynamics for benchmarking your company for top performance.

Rate Your Company on Each of the 33 Dynamics as You Read Each Chapter

In the following 33 short chapters, we provide a description and business case examples of the Gold Medal Level corporate performance for each of the 33 dynamics.

A unique feature of this book is the practical self-rating tool at the end of each chapter that offers you an opportunity to rate your own company on the dynamic covered in that chapter. For example, turn to pages *16 to 17* and take a look at the last two pages of "Dynamic One—Plan Strategically." You will see that this self-rating tool presents a concise description of all six levels found in companies for that dynamic:

1. "Endangered Survivor Level"
2. "Struggling Survivor Level"
3. "Enduring Survivor Level"
4. "Bronze Medal Level"
5. "Silver Medal Level"
6. "Gold Medal Level"

After reading that chapter and the self-rating descriptions of all six levels, we recommend that you take the opportunity to reflect and then honestly choose the level where *your* company functions. The description of each of the six levels has a box next to it. You will also notice that under each box there is a range of numbers that represents varying degrees of company practice at that level. Thus, for the:

- ❖"Endangered Survivor Level," you can give your company a score from 1 to 5
- ❖"Struggling Survivor Level," you can give your company a score from 6 to 10
- ❖"Enduring Survivor Level," you can give your company a score from 11 to 15
- ❖"Bronze Medal Level," you can give your company a score from 16 to 20
- ❖"Silver Medal Level," you can give your company a score from 21 to 25
- ❖"Gold Medal Level," you can give your company a score from 26 to 30

For the level you selected, you can choose a number from that range that best approximates your company's position in that level—whether it be on the low side, mid-range, or high end almost reaching the next higher level. Then you can place that numerical score in the box beside the appropriate level.

In highly unusual circumstances, your company may actually be performing beyond existing industry benchmarks for the Gold Medal Level, such that your company is setting the highest benchmark for a particular dynamic. If that is the case, congratulations! In this self-rating tool, you will award yourself 5 extra points for that dynamic—for a score of 35—because you are functioning at the extraordinary "Platinum Level" for that dynamic. In that case, beneath the Gold Metal Level, write "35 points—Platinum Level." Then turn to pages 236 or 237 and enter a "35" along the bottom of the profile under the number of the dynamic for which you are at the Platinum Level. If your company is actually setting the highest benchmark at the "Platinum Level" for any dynamic, we invite you to write or email us about your accomplishment. We'd like to hear how you did it.

At the end of this book, the concluding "Epilogue" chapter will tell you how you can total your scores to find your overall company level.

After you have worked through this book and rated your company on each of the 33 dynamics, you will have a very good idea as to which dynamic areas could be profitably improved for your company. Our "Epilogue" chapter describes how 33Dynamics LLC can make a variety of sources available to you, to elevate your company to the next level. We offer specific Action Steps that other companies have taken to reach the next higher level. These Action Steps are solidly rooted in the practices of highly successful companies, in the findings of business research, and in solid time-tested practical wisdom.

The Chinese philosopher Wang Yang-min put it best when he taught, "To know and not to act is not to know."[5] Do you want to lead your company to reach higher levels of performance and profits? Then seize the challenge, learn from the best, and take decisive managerial action. There's room at the top!

GOAL ONE:

LEAD YOUR COMPANY TO THE TOP

DYNAMIC ONE

PLAN STRATEGICALLY

"Corporate strategy is what makes the corporate whole add up to more than the sum of its business unit parts."
—MICHAEL E. PORTER, Harvard Business School[1]

Top entrepreneurs and executives carefully devise strategic plans. Why? They want to effectively position their businesses for the future.

But some thoughtful executives perceptively ask, "How does a specific strategic plan help a business any better than a competent executive's day-by-day decision making alone? Really, how important is it actually to put our business strategy down on paper?"

A thought-provoking answer can be found in the words of the renowned business consultant, Philip Kotler: "It is more important to do what is strategically right than what is immediately profitable."[2]

Thirty-four-year-old Dan Cook recognizes the long-term wisdom of Dr. Kotler's advice. As the CEO of Evertech Inc., a software company providing solutions to the insurance industry, he leads his management team to plan strategically: "We have a planning meeting for our top managers once a year in Aspen, Colorado. It is a much needed time for us to get out of the hectic office environment." His group of 11 executive managers meets during the peak ski season, spending time on the slopes and reevaluating the mission and vision statements of their company. "It's important to imagine the future and determine the continually changing business environment. I ask my managers, 'Do we want to be in existence five to ten years from now; and if we do, what steps do we need to take?'"

All evidence shows that Evertech is on target to be in existence for many, many years to come because its executives plan strategically. Evertech's sales have grown 30 percent in the last year and they project 150 percent growth over the next 4 years.

When some executives think about planning, they think about acquiring new equipment for more production, or scheduling an advertising mailing. But "strategic planning" is more comprehensive than this because it focuses on definite long- or mid-term goals. Purchasing new equipment and specific advertising campaigns are just two steps toward implementing strategic plans.

Highly effective strategic planning begins with writing a clear and concise mission statement that defines why your company exists. The best mission statements are typically guided by a clear vision of what the company can become in 10 to 20 years. The mission statement helps managers, employees, and customers to visualize a shared purpose and direction that enables the company to realize its vision.

What is your company's mission? Is it merely to make a monetary profit or does it also exist to provide a unique product or service to your customers? Evidence indicates that most companies that focus exclusively on maximizing profits go out of existence within 18 years.[3]

Mission statements that enable companies to stay in existence for the long term will specify how a company's products or services will *add value*[4] to its customers and society. The very best mission statements describe how the company will create a "win-win situation" for the company's owners, employees, suppliers, customers, and the broader community.

For example, the executive leaders of Motorola developed this mission statement for the company:

> "The purpose of Motorola is to honorably serve the needs of the community by providing products and services of superior quality at a fair price to our customers; to do this so as to earn an adequate profit which is required for the total enterprise to grow; and by so doing provide the opportunity for our employees and shareholders to achieve their reasonable personal objectives."[5]

Motorola's mission statement illustrates two of the three characteristics of a good mission statement: (1) focus on a small number of basic goals, and (2) emphasis on central values and major policies towards stakeholders.

The third characteristic of a good mission statement is definition of the major competitive scope in which the company operates. The mission statement of eBay illustrates this third characteristic:

> "We help people trade practically anything on earth. We will continue to enhance the online trading experiences of all—collectors, dealers, small businesses, unique item seekers, bargain hunters, opportunity sellers, and browsers."

A good mission statement clarifies the meaning and purpose of your organization—that is, "why" your company exists. The "what" of your company consists in your products and/or services and the "how" is provided by your business strategies.

For thousands of years, highly effective leaders have recognized the need to consider the future through making strategic plans. The world's all-time best-selling book, the Bible, states it this way,

> "Suppose one of you wants to build a tower. Will he not first sit down and estimate the cost to see if he has enough money to complete it? For if he lays the foundation and is not able to finish it, everyone who sees it will ridicule

> him, saying, 'This fellow began to build and was not able to finish it.'"[6]

Companies functioning at the Gold Medal Level of strategic planning are exciting places to visit. Each employee can envision how his or her work is a positive contribution to realizing the vision and mission of the company. The enthusiastic passion of the workers is contagious and spills over to create excited customers, illustrating the enduring truth of an ancient adage, "The plans of the diligent lead to profit."[7]

One of our favorite artists is Michelangelo. We have had the pleasure of seeing many of his works in our business travel to Florence, Italy. Art critics widely agree that this statue of the Biblical character "David" is an all-time great masterpiece. We would say it is at the "Platinum Level." Out of one large piece of marble with a prominent flaw, Michelangelo had to plan strategically to work around this huge obstacle to create one of the world's most beautiful pieces of art. Michelangelo once said, "I saw the angel in the marble and carved until I set him free." Talk about a man with vision!

> *"We aim above the mark to hit the mark."*
>
> —Ralph Waldo Emerson

Dynamic One: Plan Strategically		
Score	Level	Description
☐ 1-5	Endangered Survivor Level	The company executive is so preoccupied with the day-to-day business operations that he or she does not have time to ponder why the company exists. The executive has not yet developed a strategic plan for the company.
☐ 6-10	Struggling Survivor Level	The executive considers some important future trends when making day-by-day decisions in the current business situation, but lacks a fully developed long-term strategy.
☐ 11-15	Enduring Survivor Level	The executive has developed a mental vision of how your company can be better positioned in the future.

Dynamic One: Plan Strategically		
Score	**Level**	**Description**
☐ 16-20	Bronze Medal Level	Your company has written vision and mission statements and is developing a corporate identity.
☐ 21-25	Silver Medal Level	The vision, mission, and corporate identity are documented and "lived out" consistently.
☐ 26-30	Gold Medal Level	Your company is a dynamic value-oriented organization. It continues to adapt to changes in the market environment with corporate excellence, implementing its vision, mission, corporate identity, strategy, and shared values.

Dynamic Two

Organize Through Goals

"Historically, leaders were referred to as 'captain of the ship' to denote their role in operating the vessel entrusted to their care. Future leaders must be both designers and operators. Their principle contribution will be to shape the design of the organizational structure and policies so as to best fulfill the corporate mission."

—Ray Stata, Chairman and President of Analog Devices[1]

How should you "play the game" of organizing your company? In his book, *You Can Start a Business*, Laurence Holt wrote, "The origins of the word *organization* stem from a Greek word *organon* which means a tool. So the organization is a tool to reach the company's goals."[2] Thus you "play the game" of business by working toward your goals with the "tool" of the organization of your company.

After making strategic plans, the effective executive guides the company to formulate specific goals to implement those plans. In so doing, the executive takes specific action to make sure that the company is organized the best it can be, in order to effectively reach those goals.

But all too often, executives find their companies are operating at a low, dysfunctional level. The organizational structure is so shoddy that it leaves the company endangered, unable to fully realize its goals. Typically in this situation, your own work as a business executive is driven by the urgent business of the day. You rarely have time to think about how to improve your organizational system. You just barely have enough time to keep up with your work in the existing system.

A harried manager once complained, "Sometimes I run my job, and sometimes my job runs me. Right now, it's a tie!" At this endangered level, the organizational system dictates what you do instead of you designing your organizational system to most effectively reach your goals. You follow habitual rules and procedures. Too often, such companies feel like frantic, overly busy treadmills, chaotically whirling out of control—disasters waiting to happen.

But your company isn't going to survive very long if you are just putting out fires or just trying to keep your head above water. In order to survive the rapid changes in our globalized economy, top executives organize their companies in the most effective manner to achieve the goals that follow from the corporate strategic plans. Highly effective executives "run their organizations" much more often than their "organizations run them."

Forty-four-year-old Elizabeth Sortino, the founder of a gourmet candy company called Bluelands Gourmet Candy Inc., found herself frustrated with the hectic day-to-day work of her business. She soon realized that as the CEO of a $5.4 million business, she really needed to be working on the overall business strategy to address the company's 5 to 10 year outlook rather than attending only to day-to-day operations. "I realized that I wasn't as organized as I should be. I needed to be working on process improvement and overall employee development." So two years ago, Sortino decided to hire a COO who could manage the daily business operations of the 32 employees at Blueland. She explained, "It was one of the best decisions I've made. I think a lot of the time as founders, we have a difficult time delegating responsibility to the right people in our business. But I've realized that as CEO I need to be able to step back and review our overall business strategy for success."

Here's a practical way to improve your company: Develop a picture of possible future challenges. Then strengthen your business concept by envisioning how your company could uniquely respond to those possible future challenges.

Think of your business concept as a photo taken by a reconnaissance jet. Just as you would try to decipher all the implications of a reconnaissance spy photo from a distance, try to envision future challenges to your company from afar, and consider the following issues:

- ❖What are the next milestones in developing my business concept?
- ❖What obstacles might we encounter in the future?
- ❖What ideas do we need to abandon?
- ❖Which resources will be needed?
- ❖How should my company be organized to best implement our business concept?

At the Gold Medal Level, well thought out mid-term and long-term goals are continually readjusted to reposition your company to optimally respond to the market place. In organizing your company, it is vitally important to create a structure that promotes employee involvement in this continual goal setting to achieve your strategic plans.

When a manager collaboratively negotiates a reasonable goal for a worker, it influences that employee's belief in their ability to accomplish the task. A manager should negotiate *specific*, challenging high-performance goals for employees that are neither too low nor too high. And the employee's positive belief in their ability to accomplish their goals will enhance their work performance.[3]

Once goals are set, your ongoing organizational structure should provide regular feedback to all employees on their progress toward the goals. The company organization should incorporate supervisory feedback to every employee about their work accomplishments in terms of the performance goals that are mutually set.[4]

> *"For when the one Great Scorer comes to write against your name, he marks—not that you won or lost-but how you played the game."*
>
> —GRANTLAND RICE, a sports commentator[5]

Dynamic Two: Organize Through Goals		
Score	**Level**	**Description**
☐ 1-5	Endangered Survivor Level	The work of the executive managers of your company is driven by the urgent business of the day. As a result, you rarely have time to think about how to improve your organizational system. You just barely have enough time to keep up with your work in the existing system.
☐ 6-10	Struggling Survivor Level	Well-intended plans may exist, but specific strategic goals have not been set. Therefore, short-term activities still take precedence over taking actions designed for long-term success. Urgent tasks crowd out important tasks.
☐ 11-15	Enduring Survivor Level	Executive managers in your company set annual business goals based on top priorities. Thus you lead your company with strategic thinking.

Dynamic Two: Organize Through Goals		
Score	**Level**	**Description**
☐ 16-20	Bronze Medal Level	In addition to annual goal-setting, mid-term strategic planning is used in the company. Thus executive managers effectively project goals for the next 2-3 years.
☐ 21-25	Silver Medal Level	Company executives have established long-term goals that extend 5 or more years into the future.
☐ 26-30	Gold Medal Level	Well thought out mid-term and long-term goals are continually readjusted to reposition your company to best respond to the marketplace.

Dynamic Three

Lead to Success

"...we are beginning to see that traditional autocratic and hierarchical modes of leadership are slowly yielding to a newer model—one that attempts to simultaneously enhance the personal growth of workers and improve the quality and caring of our many institutions through a combination of teamwork and community, personal involvement in decision making, and ethical and caring behavior. This emerging approach to leadership and service is called servant-leadership."

—Larry Spears, CEO of Greenleaf Center, founded by Robert Greenleaf[1]

Some say that certain people are "born" leaders. But this isn't really the case. Although some personalities are thought to be the natural "leadership type," many individuals can develop certain traits, attributes, and behaviors that make a great leader.

In November 1875, H. J. Heinz at the age of 31 was $2,000 in debt and "had not a penny." Nevertheless, he launched a business that initially prospered. But then Heinz faced a devastating cash flow problem. He had expanded too quickly without having adequate financing lined up. So his company went bankrupt. This made Heinz personally liable for $20,000. Because the dollar in the 1870's was worth far more than its value today, this represented a huge personal debt.

But this new setback didn't faze him. The very next year, Heinz launched another food company with a ketchup product line. This time Heinz carefully managed his cash flow and the rest is a well-known history of his company's extraordinary success.[2]

Frankly, H. J. Heinz was not a "born leader." But he did learn significant leadership skills through some tough experiences. Business researchers at the Greenleaf Center concluded,

> "Leadership seems to be the marshaling of skills possessed by a majority but used by a minority. But it's something that can be learned by anyone, taught to everyone, denied to no one."[3]

Effective executive leaders master four major management skills through their training and experience:

1. *Planning* involves selecting a source of action and specifying how the action will be implemented.
2. *Organizing* involves creatively structuring the company's workforce to maximize performance.
3. *Directing and motivating* involves mobilizing people to carry out plans and run routine operations.
4. *Controlling* involves ensuring that the plan is actually carried out and is appropriately modified as circumstances change.[4]

Great leaders effectively join forces with others to reach company goals, thereby setting themselves apart from the mediocre or even the typical good leaders.[5]

Successful executive leaders communicate their vision so clearly and persuasively that others adopt that vision as part of their own. The more others follow you, the greater your influence and the stronger your leadership.

Tragically, history tells of the huge impact of highly influential but horribly evil leaders such as Adolf Hitler, Joseph Stalin, and Saddam Hussein. And history similarly documents the decisive effects of powerful, but highly corrupt *business* leaders. So true greatness is *not* measured by the sheer degree of one's influence.

Instead, a mark of a truly great leader is the worthiness of one's goals, pursued in a highly ethical manner. So admirable leadership boils down to *effectively influencing others to attain a worthy goal.*

Setting him or her apart from others, a great leader displays numerous characteristics simultaneously. He or she:

- ❖has a worthy vision for the company,
- ❖formulates and implements excellent strategies,
- ❖brings out the best in his or her workforce,
- ❖gets things done effectively,
- ❖seizes opportunities,
- ❖creates a sustainable competitive advantage,
- ❖launches new businesses,
- ❖builds organizations,
- ❖masters important details that could make or break the company, and
- ❖permeates every action with consistently high ethical standards.[6]

For example, when a moral dilemma surfaces, such as an unanticipated product defect, a great leader does not hesitate to resolve the matter immediately in favor of the consumer.[7]

At the very top "Gold Medal Level" of corporate leadership, this highly ethical and effective executive action is called "Servant Leadership." In his book, *Servant As Leader*, Robert Greenleaf described servant leadership in this way:

> "The servant-leader is servant first.... It begins with the natural feeling that one wants to serve, to serve first. Then conscious choice brings one to aspire to lead. He or she is sharply different from the person who is leader first, perhaps because of the need to assuage an unusual power drive or to acquire material possessions. The leader-first and the servant-first are two extreme types. The difference manifests itself in the care taken by the servant-first to make sure that other people's highest priority needs are being served."[8]

Knowing that the leader's most noble role is to serve others, the most effective executives promote fairness, compassion, listening, teamwork, trust, integrity, and the proper use of power and empowerment.

Centuries before the famous contemporary business research of Robert Greenleaf, the Bible conveyed this same truth, "He shall be greatest who is servant of all."[9] And, "Each of you should look not only to your own interests, but also to the interest of others."[10]

In his best-selling book, *Good to Great,* Jim Collins reported his recent research into good-to-great companies. The good-to-great leaders were constantly described with words such as "quiet, humble, modest, reserved, shy, gracious, mild-mannered, self-effacing, understated, did not believe his own clippings; and so forth."[11]

As a matter of fact, eleven of the good-to-great CEOs were some of the most outstanding leaders of the century who drew so little attention to themselves that very few people know anything about them. "How many of these extraordinary executives have you heard of? George Cain, Alan Wurtzel, David Maxwell, Colman Mockler, Darwin Smith, Jim Herring, Lyle Everingham, Joe Cullman, Fred Allen, Cork Walgreen, and Carl Reichardt."[12] These CEOs were just "…seemingly ordinary people quietly producing extraordinary results,"[13] writes Collins.

Servant leadership[14] is a very practical philosophy that teaches that greatness is a secondary by-product of supporting other people's needs first. Great leaders create "win-win" conditions in their companies for their stockholders, customers, employees, and suppliers.

> *"Enhance the long-term viability of the enterprise—resist the short-term scorecard in a manner which balances short- and long-term interests."*
>
> —Maureen McNulty, Stanford University's Graduate School of Business[15]

Dynamic Three: Lead to Success		
Score	**Level**	**Description**
☐ 1-5	Endangered Survivor Level	The company owners or board has elevated a corporate executive to a leadership position before that person has learned much about what it takes to be an effective business leader.
☐ 6-10	Struggling Survivor Level	The executive is on the way to mastering some leadership qualities, but lacks a focused vision for the company. And the owners and/or board of directors have not clearly defined the company vision.
☐ 11-15	Enduring Survivor Level	The executive is developing a vision. But every-day business activities take precedence over sharpening that vision and systematically pursuing it.

Dynamic Three: Lead to Success		
Score	**Level**	**Description**
☐ 16-20	Bronze Medal Level	The executive leads with a clearly articulated vision for the company. The executive uses power appropriately and ethically.
☐ 21-25	Silver Medal Level	The executive leads in a highly ethical manner and manifests nearly all the personal traits and skills of an effective leader. The vast majority of the employees of the company follow his/her leadership.
☐ 26-30	Gold Medal Level	The executive is a servant leader who demonstrates all the effective traits and behaviors of a great leader. He or she continually develops his/her leadership style to serve all the stakeholders of the company ethically and with great effectiveness.

Dynamic Four

Control to Profit

"It is not only the process of timely measurement, but what we as managers do with that measurement."

—Chuck Weindruck, Controller of Westwood Industries

Chuck Weindruck recognizes the vital necessity for managers to obtain and act on accurate, up-to-date data. Why is this so vital? Because it empowers the executive to regulate the allocation of company resources to maximize the company's performance and resultant profits.

Every diligent entrepreneur and executive should strive to manage the company to generate the healthiest profit for the owner or shareholders. About 30 centuries ago, an ancient book of wisdom endorsed both the profit motive and commended its necessary prerequisite, "The plans of the diligent lead to profit as surely as haste leads to poverty."[1]

This wisdom still holds true. Making managerial decisions in haste without diligently planning to implement adequate control systems risks irreparable damage to companies.

Some experienced engineers recently spoke to us. They are employed by a small engineering firm—which we will call XYZ Corporation. They described numerous company problems that all boil down to habitual inattention to control issues by the company's executives.

XYZ Corporation apparently lacked an adequate cost accounting system, if they had any cost accounting system at all. XYZ's executives would frequently outbid other engineering firms with the lowest bids for contracts. These executives regularly submitted bids for projects for which they had not specifically projected any realistic calculations on how much time the project would actually take to complete. They also neglected to conduct any specific cost analysis to estimate with any degree of accuracy the actual personnel, materials, and overhead costs required to fulfill the contract. Apparently, the only matter of concern to the XYZ Corporation executives was that they receive the contract to boost their company's current revenue.

Because of XYZ Corporation's lack of controls, they increasingly had to delay promised deliveries. Typically, the executives would encounter major cash flow problems because they had grossly underestimated the costs and time required to fulfill a contract. Then the executive's solution would be to lay off some staff, abruptly cut the remaining employees' salaries, demand that those employees work longer hours for reduced pay to complete the contracted project, and then hurriedly go out bidding for new contracts to obtain the capital necessary to complete past contracts. Because this was not just an isolated case but a repeated managerial pattern, employee morale was severely undermined.

Without an adequate internal control system to provide a more efficient operation, XYZ Corporation has been on the brink of bankruptcy several times. With little control, the company has no way to anticipate whether they will produce a profit from quarter to quarter. Now, the very existence of the firm depends on the firm's ability to keep landing new contracts before engineering staff has completed past contracts. This further encourages underbidding to land those contracts in a hurry to solve chronic cash flow problems. XYZ Corporation is like a house of cards that could collapse at any moment, as it deservedly acquires a reputation for delayed deliveries, and as it risks getting so far behind that its engineers could never complete the accumulated unfinished projects. Clearly, the long-term viability of XYZ Corporation is now very much in doubt because it has neglected to control for profit.

It has been said that *planning* and *control* are the "Siamese twins of management."[2] Professors Bateman and Snell defined "control" as "[t]he process of measuring progress toward planned performance and applying corrective measures to ensure that performance is in line with managers' objectives."[3] The primary control function is to ensure that their plans and strategies are carried out properly. If employees, vendors, or subcontractors are not doing what needs to be done to implement strategic plans, then managers must promptly take action to correct the situation.

Most managers today realize that they must perform in an environment of rapid changes. Clearly, it is not sufficient to merely check on the condition of one's business periodically. Managers taking this passive approach will eventually discover that it is too late to be able to rescue their business that has declined by their neglect to control.

Successful managers do not limit themselves to mere gut feelings about the condition of their business. Instead, the managers who maximize profits are those who implement systems for achieving organizational control. These systems provide the real time data and warning signs they need to make corrective action.

"I once thought that just because I was making a profit that I was doing things right," commented Scott Slawinski, founder and CEO of EngineCore Inc. "The financial figures looked great, until you compared them to the industry averages." Now Slawinski is known for his industry "piranhas." Sent out in teams, they work together finding out how the industry is doing as a whole, researching and analyzing what their competition is doing. Slawinski jokingly replied when asked about how his business is doing now, "We are tearing up the competition!" With over $75 million in sales growth in the past 5 years, his statement is figuratively true. He clearly moved his company from the dangers of surviving on annual financial statements alone, to one with formal control systems designed to continuously measure more meaningful progress toward planned performance.

Planned performance involves setting performance standards. Standards are performance targets for a given goal. Standards should be set for all the company's important activities, whether they are financial, legal, operations, charity, etc. Performance standards are typically set with regard to:

- ❖quality (such as stringent limits on defects),
- ❖quantity (such as dollars, or volume of output),
- ❖cost (such as expenditure for materials and labor),
- ❖time used (such as on-time delivery of finished, and product).

Finally, once you reach the Gold Medal Level, in addition to real-time formal control system information, much control is achieved through the trust and shared values of company employees. At this highest level, you may no longer need to rely solely on real-time formal control systems. Instead, you empower your employees to make sound judgments in decision-making because they share the core values, goals, and expectation of the organization. You have built strong relationships of trust and respect with your employees and you have encouraged them to take responsibility for their own actions. You have communicated so thoroughly with your employees and know them so well that you fully trust that they are keeping the organization's best interests at heart. Therefore, there is an environment where both the executives and the employees are in a "win-win situation." There is group cohesiveness in the shared accomplishment of both formal and informal controls to maximize company profits.

"All that we do is done with an eye to something else."

—ARISTOTLE[4]

Dynamic Four: Control to Profit		
Score	**Level**	**Description**
☐ 1-5	Endangered Survivor Level	No control system exists. Management has only checkbook balances, annual balances, and annual tax returns on which to make managerial decisions.
☐ 6-10	Struggling Survivor Level	You create a formal annual financial statement, but you recognize the need to compare company performance to standards using criteria beyond annual ratio analysis of profitability and liquidity.
☐ 11-15	Enduring Survivor Level	You have progressed to using monthly or quarterly evaluation reports to monitor the financial position of your company.

Dynamic Four: Control to Profit		
Score	**Level**	**Description**
☐ 16-20	Bronze Medal Level	On both quarterly and monthly schedules, you measure performance to compare it to company performance standards. The management usually takes prompt corrective action where significant variances are discovered.
☐ 21-25	Silver Medal Level	On a weekly or "real time" basis, control systems provide all levels of management with measures of performance that are compared to past performance.
☐ 26-30	Gold Medal Level	In addition to using real-time formal control system information, much control is achieved through the trust and shared values of company employees.

Dynamic Five

Require Ethical Excellence

"Ethical business is good for you and good for profits too!"
—Laurence Holt, management consultant,
and Senior Research Fellow,
University of Reading, U.K.[1]

A solid ethical foundation is necessary for making sound decisions throughout your entire company. Ethical issues arise in every area of your business, whether it be with your customers, suppliers, employees, or the community.

Certainly, you don't want your suppliers to cheat you with inferior products that fail to meet your agreed-upon specifications. And you wouldn't be pleased if that supplier made delivery promises to you that they knew they were unable to fulfill. With a lack of integrity, fairness, and compassion, a supplier might get an initial order from you, but such a short-sighted approach ultimately fails in the long run because you will look for an ethical supplier for your next order.

A good moral judgment is (1) logical, (2) based on relevant facts, and (3) based on sound moral principles.[2] A famous Judeo-Christian principle is "...love your neighbor as yourself,"[3] or phrased as the "Golden Rule"—"Do unto others as you would have them do unto you." The Judeo-Christian ethical principles of love, justice, and holiness exist because they reflect aspects of God's character. In Western business, these three ethical principles are often described as *compassion, fairness,* and *integrity.*[4]

When baking a cake, you need all the right ingredients, such as flower, yeast, and eggs, to make the cake taste good. When making ethical business decisions, the three essential ingredients that must be combined in the "recipe" are integrity, fairness, and compassion.

- ❖ If you made all your decisions with integrity but lacked fairness and compassion, you would drift into impersonal legalism.
- ❖ If you made decisions based only on fairness, without including integrity and compassion, you would produce harsh outcomes.
- ❖ And if you were to make all decisions based only on compassion, you would lack an adequate moral compass.

That's why all three "ingredients" are essential to be truly ethical.

Are the highly publicized corporate scandals typical of Western business practice? Archie Dunham, the CEO of ConocoPhillips, told us in 2002 that massive ethical failures by corporate executives represent only a few "rotten apples" in a large barrel of apples. Mr. Dunham reported his experience that the vast majority of American corporate executives do not practice the gross unethical behavior of Enron and WorldCom in the U.S., and Ahold and Parmalat in Europe. While many cultures and even governments in the world routinely practice bribery, dishonesty, and corruption in business dealings, the vast majority of corporate executives in the United States try to conduct business ethically for three reasons:

- ❖ They are aware that numerous laws are in place and are strictly enforced by government and private lawsuits.
- ❖ They are coasting on the memory of a Judeo-Christian ethic.
- ❖ They recognize that ethical business enhances customer satisfaction and long-term profits.

Companies with shabby and downright deplorable unethical practices do "succeed" in terms of unfairly reaping profits. Even outright crime often pays—otherwise there would be far fewer criminals. Down through human history, dishonest businesspeople have swindled, defrauded, deceived, and otherwise unfairly short-changed their customers.

But a perceptive proverb contains a practical warning, "The integrity of the upright guides them, but the unfaithful are destroyed by their duplicity."[5] So there is a self-preservation motive for conducting business at the highest levels of ethical excellence.

Another ancient proverb says, "The Lord abhors dishonest scales, but accurate weights are his delight."[6] Even if no one else sees you cheat, it's an awesome reality that God observes everything we do. Eventually, we'll all have to account for our actions to Him.

It has been said, "If we are unwilling to account for our actions publicly, we are probably doing something wrong." A scripture states, "...men loved darkness instead of light because their deeds were evil."[7] When people do something wrong, they prefer to perform their deeds in the dark—in secret—rather than in public in full view of everyone. Why? One hopes to get away with a wrong action when it is done in the dark. The businessperson who is unwilling to give a full public account of an action is likely trying to hide motives and actions because they are wrong.

Tony Simons had this to say about integrity, "The notion that behavioral integrity is important should be common sense: Align your words and actions in a way employees see. Keep your promises. It seems simple, but if it's so simple, why is it so rarely observed?"[8]

Ed Puckhaber M.B.A., a top executive of Morgan Stanley Dean Witter, told us that he made it a practice to hold meetings on ethical compliance every six months with all the managers and professionals reporting to him. Each time he emphasized that all employees are required to behave with the highest ethical standards. He reviewed the ethical standards that must be followed, making it clear that if a business situation ever arose in which the employee was uncertain about the ethical course of action, that employee should promptly review the matter with him and/or the legal department.

This approach has been highly effective in preventing ethical lapses by his subordinates. The regular meetings on ethical standards every six months served as a regular reminder to his staff that Puckhaber expected ethical excellence.

Once you have risen to the Silver Medal Level, senior managers periodically emphasize to all employees that they must abide by the Company's Code of Ethics. All managers apply integrity, fairness, and compassion to all of their decision-making. Managers not only actively implement and promote the Code of Ethics, but they also *lead by example.*

At the Gold Medal Level, senior managers implement regular practical training in business ethics throughout the whole company and have a system to monitor and rapidly enforce the corporate Code of Ethics. "Good understanding wins favor, but the way of the unfaithful is hard."[9] Executive managers must deliberately teach all employees to apply the highest ethical principles to everyday decisions.

Every decision at every level of the organization is evaluated with the three values of integrity, fairness, and compassion. At this level, senior managers actively involve subordinates in evaluating business ethics cases to give them practice in dealing with ethical cases in the company. Management actively supports ethical decisions.

The result is a corporate culture that expects highly ethical business practices. Infused with the highest ethical values, this corporate culture becomes much more powerful than any mere Code of Ethics can be. Executives and other managers model highly ethical behavior. The clear expectation it that all business will be highly ethical. All company employees come to monitor one another, creating an ingrained accountability check on one another. Beyond adhering to the "letter of the law" of a Code of Ethics, a highly ethical corporate culture promotes business that follows the true "spirit of the law."

A Jewish leader explained, "Two central principles provide the foundation for all of our business activities: *tsedek* (fairness and justice), and *chessed* (goodness). In other words, one should follow not only the letter of the law, but the spirit of the law *(lifnim mishurat hadin)*"[10]

Some years ago, a criminal tampered with Tylenol, causing the public to distrust the product's purity. Although it was not the company's fault, the executives of Johnson & Johnson swiftly recalled all Tylenol bottles from shelves across the country at a loss of millions of dollars. They quickly engineered a tamper-proof package that would make it obvious if anyone had opened the bottles, and then restocked America's shelves with newly packaged Tylenol. These swift, consumer-protective actions gained the company great respect and trust, resulting in a rebounding of sales of Tylenol. That was great executive leadership! High ethics produced eventual high profits.

The actions of Jim Burke, CEO of Johnson & Johnson, were prompted by his own strong personal character and by the ethical values imbedded in the corporate culture. This is what he said about how he handled the crisis:

> "If you look at the Tylenol situation, the reason that the country was so responsive was not really me, it was because the company I represented had a hundred years of relationships with the public and had built a sense of trust. What they were doing by trusting demonstrated that they believed in the character of Johnson & Johnson, a character that had been epitomized by all of its leadership. But beyond that it was very central to the company to be concerned about all of their constituencies and to recognize, through a document we all live by called the "Credo," that those constituencies are interrelated and that we are in business to serve society, and if you did that well you ended up making more money for your stockholders over the long run."[11]

Johnson & Johnson is famous for its corporate culture of strong ethics. Those exemplary ethics produced an almost automatic correct response to the Tylenol crisis. And those ethics produced even greater good will and profits.

While Enron was destroyed by executives failing to behave ethically, Johnson & Johnson thrives as a highly profitable company because of its corporate culture of integrity, fairness, and compassion.

Gustav von Hertzen concluded, "Long-term economic stability and growth is rare. Where it has been seen, there has always been a strong ethical and moral component in that society."[12]

Clearly, your company will greatly benefit from adhering to sound ethical standards.

> *"We have spent five thousand years as a race of rational human beings trying to drag ourselves out of the primeval slime by searching for truth...and moral absolutes. In the place of Truth we have discovered facts; for moral absolutes we have substituted moral ambiguity....Our society finds Truth too strong a medicine to digest undiluted. In its purest form Truth is not a polite tap on the shoulder; it is a howling reproach. What Moses brought down from Mount Sinai were not the Ten Suggestions...they are Commandments. The sheer brilliance of the Ten Commandments is that they codify, in a handful of words, acceptable human behavior. Not just for then...or now...but for all time."*
>
> —TED KOPPEL, ABC television news anchor, in a 1987 speech to students at Duke University[13]

Dynamic Five: Require Ethical Excellence		
Score	**Level**	**Description**
☐ 1-5	Endangered Survivor Level	Ethics are never or rarely discussed in the company.
☐ 6-10	Struggling Survivor Level	Senior management attends to ethical issues as if they were matters secondary to making a profit. Only one of the three core ethical principles (integrity, fairness, or compassion) is sometimes used in decision-making.
☐ 11-15	Enduring Survivor Level	Senior management recognizes the importance of ethics and discusses ethical issues with employees on occasion as they arise. Usually, just one or two of the three core ethical principles (integrity, fairness, and compassion) are used in business decision-making.

Dynamic Five: Require Ethical Excellence		
Score	**Level**	**Description**
☐ 16-20	Bronze Medal Level	Senior management has written a corporate Code of Ethics and has distributed it to all employees. Integrity, fairness, and compassion are required principles to be applied in decision-making.
☐ 21-25	Silver Medal Level	Senior managers periodically emphasize to all employees that they must abide by the written Code of Ethics of the company. They have a system to monitor and rapidly enforce the Code of Ethics. All managers regularly apply integrity, fairness, and compassion to their making-decisions.
☐ 26-30	Gold Medal Level	In addition to regular practical training in business ethics throughout the entire company, your firm's corporate culture is infused with the highest ethical values. All managers model adherence to the three principles of integrity, fairness, and compassion in all their relationships and decision-making. All employees monitor one another, keeping each other ethically accountable.

Dynamic Six

Balance Your Managerial Life

"Life is like juggling crystal balls and rubber balls, and success depends on knowing which is which. My crystal balls are my religion, my faith, my work in this country. Everything else is a rubber ball. You can let it drop, wait for a week or month, let it bounce. Life is about choices. Life is about balance."

—Roy Roberts, a Vice President of General Motors Corporation[1]

We have only one life, but we live in three overlapping worlds—our business world, our family world, and our other social world. Imagine bringing your spouse and kids to a meeting with seven of your salespersonnel. Sitting off to your left, Miss Wright asks the question on the minds of all her fellow sales colleagues, "Why did you bring your family to our meeting today? Will they be playing any sort of role in our discussion?" You simply respond, "No, they're just here so I can tend to their needs."

Of course, this is a highly unlikely scenario. You don't bring your family into work with you every day. However, Heather Howitt does. Howitt, the CEO of Oregon Chai in Portland, Oregon, balances motherhood with her responsibility of running an eleven million dollar manufacturer of tea lattes. "Our office is a very casual place. We've got a family element going on here."

Living in the rain soaked city of Portland, 32-year-old Howitt often arrives at her office lightly splattered with mud. She often spends her lunch break taking her one-year-old son, Sawyer, to a nearby park, or to her nanny who takes him home. On other days, she simply places him in his crib in her office.

With the growth of her company, Howitt hired some key executives including a chief operating officer to manage operations and finance. She also delegated the sales calls that she used to make herself. "I used to come in at 6 a.m. and make calls nonstop," she explained. "I don't have to do that anymore." Howitt positioned herself in a way so that she is no longer personally over-worked or over-challenged by her daily responsibilities at the company. She balanced her business and private life. She not only recognized her strategic contribution to the success of Oregon Chai, but she also appreciates her unique role in the life of her young son.[2]

As an entrepreneur or a business executive, you must give your best in two entirely different worlds. The needs of your business and the needs of your family and friends compete for your time and attention. And both expect the very best from you. Heather Howitt found one way to do it; you may have another way.

To enjoy both the rewards of business success and family fulfillment, you need to constantly work to keep your balance. To successfully tackle the challenges of a fast-growing company, you need all the personal resources that come from a balanced life. "How do you develop a balanced business personality?"

Some entrepreneurial executives suffer from dangerous imbalance. Others achieve top excellence in maintaining optimal balance. "Early in my career, I use to think that entrepreneurship was more an art than a science, that it was a gift or something," says Cherrill Farnsworth. "I don't believe that anymore."[3] Entrepreneurial leadership is not some automatic personality trait or some artistic talent some people are just born with and others happen to lack. Instead, entrepreneurial effectiveness with a balanced life is a dynamic process that you must constantly work at. If you don't keep developing and nurturing your entrepreneurial personality, it might just die. Then, only drastic action might revive that entrepreneurial spirit.

That's exactly what happened to Sam T. Goodner. His software company, the Austin-based Catapult Systems Corp., ranked 77th among the fastest growing companies in America while Goodner served as the founding CEO. At age 33, Goodner decided to step down as CEO of Catapult to take on the new challenge of serving as CEO of Inquisite Inc., a Catapult subsidiary that sells software over the Internet. But Goodner soon found his new digs to be "harsher, more spartan" than what he was accustomed to. "Half of it is actually under ground," he explained, describing his much less attractive new office space.

But Goodner was not complaining. After all, it was his own idea to leave the comfortable CEO position of Catapult with a staff of 115, to head Inquisite Inc., with only 20 employees. But now something was wrong. To be sure, there were plenty of challenges to attend to. The phone rang for his attention, paper kept filling the "in" box, and email messages steadily came in from employees, venders, and customers. Every day, and every hour, urgent decisions had to be made, so much so that anyone in his shoes could have been overwhelmed by the "tyranny of the urgent."

But increasingly, he felt like he was only reacting to demands and not taking a visionary proactive role any longer. And too often, long hours of work would crowd out what he'd prefer to do in his home and personal life. Even worse, he realized that even if he could experience any gratification in his personal world, it could not make up for what was missing in his business world.

"I had none of my entrepreneurial creativity left," Goodner reflected. "I was falling back on what was easy. You know that's happening when you start just going through your email all day long." Recognizing that his former entrepreneurial spirit was gone, he resigned and hired a new CEO to head the company.

Perhaps Goodner had already achieved financial independence and had other worthy goals to pursue in life. In that case, relinquishing his CEO position could be the best decision to make. But could there have been another way to recover his entrepreneurial spirit with a healthy balance of attention to work, family, and friends?[4]

Entrepreneurial functioning can range from the low level, "You are personally over worked and over challenged"—to the most desirable level, "You regularly implement action plans to improve every aspect of your life."

The lowest level of functioning leaves your company endangered. Top management is personally over worked and over challenged. The unrelenting urgent matters of your business seem to demand so much of your time that you go to work earlier and earlier, and stay later and later into the evening. You are like a runaway tire, rolling down a steep hill, turning faster and faster and faster until finally, you run out of control and then crash.

Or, you might think of it this way: The underlying foundation of your life at work and at home is built on sand instead of a solid rock. Even the slightest storm will plunge you into a danger area, damaging your relationships with your business associates and with your family and friends.

You are barely surviving, but you are endangered like a stick of dynamite that has been lit; you don't have much time before things will blow up in your business, or in your family life, or in both. You must get out as soon as possible. But how? You can't help but think, "There must be a better way." And you are right! There is.

An ancient Hebrew writing warns, "In vain you rise early and stay up late, toiling for food to eat—for he [the Lord God] grants sleep to those he loves."[5] God, who created our reality, designed us and the world for a better set of options.

"Over the past three years, I've been able to identify gradually what things I can give to my CPA, or to my bookkeeper, or to my office manager. I read about people who work 60 or 90 hours a week and build multimillion-dollar businesses at the expense of their health and family. Those aren't success stories in my book. Success is having a multimillion-dollar business and the other stuff, too," says 40-year-old

Tom Melaragno, founder of the $7.6-million Compri Consulting, an IT consulting and staffing firm founded in 1992. Although he put in 12-hour days when he started the business, today he works just 8 or 9 hours and makes sure he's there to watch his two sons' Little League baseball games in the summer and coach the older one's football team in the fall.[6]

Taking a proactive stance means you take control to invest your life wisely. Scott Tinley is an extraordinary triathlete who has competed in more than 350 triathlons including 19 Hawaii Ironman triathlons. The triathlon is an endurance sport involving swimming, bicycling, and running. Amazingly, Tinley has won nearly 100 races.

"This sport is about a combination of personal challenge, camaraderie, and achievement of self-knowledge," Tinley explains.

Tinley is more than just an athlete; he is also a successful entrepreneur. He co-founded a company that produced athletic clothing—Tinley Performance Wear. He and his partners built the business over 8 years, reaching about $10 million in sales. In 1992, they sold the company to Reebok. But even more than just being a triathlete and a wealthy businessman, Tinley is also appreciated as a writer, traveler, father, and husband. As productive as he is in many areas of life, he has not lost sight of the balance he needs.

Tinley explains the work-life balance he maintained over his 20-year career as an athlete, husband, father, and entrepreneur: "A lot of people have this image of self-management, that it means you have to drive yourself and force yourself to get things done without somebody looking over your shoulder. It is actually quite the opposite: You have to force yourself to have balance in your life and be efficient in all things you do."[7]

He has recognized the importance of what he calls a "precarious balance between preparation, competition, professionalism, support systems, and the world of family, friends, and paying the rent." He has not lost sight of the fact that among the best things in life are family, friends, and a quiet run in the park.

This is the kind of balance that John Chambers, CEO of Cisco Systems has also achieved. An interviewer, asked, "What would you like to have accomplished and what's next after Cisco?"

"The most important thing to me is my family, and that doesn't change. My wife of 25 years is a perfect balance for me. When I get down, which I occasionally do, she brings me up, and on rare occasions if I get a little bit too confident she brings me back down to earth too."

"I've got two kids I'm tremendously proud of and they are my life; so my family is first, second, and third in terms of my priorities. And when I'm at home, as my wife reminds me when I walk in the door, I'm not the CEO anymore. So at home, I'm like anybody else. Carrying out the garbage, changing the light bulbs, and so on."

"And what will I do after this? I will teach when I retire. I think giving back to the community is the right thing to do. It'd be terrible to be perhaps the most successful company in history and not give back. So I'm not going to go work for another company after Cisco. When I retire from Cisco, I'm done with the business world and I will probably go teach. Young people are so much fun to interface with.... How do you teach ethics, and how do you teach integrity earlier on? To do that would just be a blast!"[8]

Chambers illustrates how a proper balance between one's executive performance and other dimensions of life can contribute to both personal fulfillment and business success. An awareness of the need for balance has prompted many executives to make some crucial decisions in their day-to-day business and personal life that protected them from failure so they could just become an "enduring survivor."

But, no doubt, you want more from life than just maintaining a mere survivor level. You want to excel as an executive leader, and also thrive, not merely survive, in your personal life. So beyond the awareness that comes from self-assessment and evaluation of your priorities, there are additional steps to take in order to reach the top level of having all that life can offer.

Forty-year-old Mark Holland is the founder of a thriving company, Ascend HR Solutions. At the beginning of every workweek he pulls out a message that reads: "Wendi is the most important person in my life. My family comes before work and other activities. I live my religion. I provide the financial security for my family. Our home is a retreat from the challenges of the world. I have a positive attitude, looking for and developing the strength in others. I help people develop and grow, including, when appropriate, holding them accountable. The outdoors provide a needed sanctuary and retreat for me."

Holland wrote this personal mission statement in 1998 following a major crisis in his business. That year the firm lost $800,000, which caused significant problems in his partnership. Holland experienced so much stress that he lost nearly 20 pounds.

Then a business seminar inspired him to write down his life mission statement. Holland admits that the seminar gave him "a good smack upside the head." He resolved to never again sacrifice his family and health for the sake of his business.

Over a two-year period, Holland's personal mission statement grew into a life plan for himself and his wife. "We asked, 'What are the important things? What do we want to have happen before we die?'" Now they have a 30-year planned life itinerary on a spreadsheet that covers college savings, retirement, vacations, exercise regiments, relating to God and spiritual activities, work goals, personal growth, and personal relationships.

At this stage, Holland had reached the Silver Medal Level, by regularly pursuing clear, written personal goals and life motto. Writing down your personal goals and a life motto not only helps you clarify the kind of balance you want to achieve, but also gives you a written reference to check week by week. Many people refine their goals and motto over several year's time.

But Mark Holland and his wife, Wendi moved up to an even higher level. They take long walks together at least twice a week with their two-year-old daughter on Mark's shoulders and their five-month-old son snuggled in Wendi's front pack. Once a month, on one of those walks, they discuss and review their life plan thoroughly. "The plan is dynamic—it changes. It's been really good for getting our relationship and our lives back to where they needed to be," Holland says.[9]

This practice of regularly reviewing their life plan indicates that Holland progressed to the Gold Medal Level. At this top level, you constantly implement action plans to improve the balance of all five dimensions of your life.

Paul N. Howell, CEO of Howell Corporation, named an additional crucial characteristic of a successfully balanced entrepreneurial executive:

"The willingness and demonstrated ability to conduct him—or herself—on a high moral and ethical level in both business and personal life. Without it, success is uncertain and short lived."[10]

At the Gold Medal Level, people who interact with you can see the sterling qualities of your servant leadership. Your executive actions are guided by clear plans that continually balance and rebalance all the dimensions of successful living:

1. *Executive Success:* Servant leadership, management skills, and career development.
2. *Loving Relationships:* Serving family, friends, and the needy.
3. *Healthy Lifestyle:* Regular exercise, good diet, and regular medical care.
4. *Emotional Well-being:* Stress management, recreation, and psychological stability.
5. *Spiritual Maturity:* Ethical character, commitment to ultimate values, peace with God, and devoting oneself to life's greatest spiritual priorities.

At this Gold Medal Level, you regularly "retreat" from your usual executive responsibilities to rethink your personal mission, vision, and action plans. You deliberately make a continual concerted effort to maintain the delicate balance you need for a fulfilling life.

"Men for the sake of getting a living forget to live."

—Margaret Fuller

Dynamic Six: Balance Your Managerial Life		
Score	Level	Description
☐ 1-5	Endangered Survivor Level	Top management is personally over worked and over challenged.
☐ 6-10	Struggling Survivor Level	Some aspects of executive management may work satisfactorily, but there is still much room for improvement. The work of the executives often involves such long hours and stress that areas of their personal life are short-changed.
☐ 11-15	Enduring Survivor Level	Senior managers are more aware of the need to balance all the dimensions of work, social, physical, emotional, and spiritual life. Executives have set short-term business goals and have set some immediate managerial and personal priorities based on core competencies and personal values.

Dynamic Six: Balance Your Managerial Life		
Score	Level	Description
☐ 16-20	Bronze Medal Level	Many areas of senior managers' lives are coming into balance and harmony. A balanced lifestyle is beginning to be achieved.
☐ 21-25	Silver Medal Level	Executives in your company regularly pursue clear, written personal goals and a life motto that guides a balanced managerial and personal life.
☐ 26-30	Gold Medal Level	Senior managers regularly review and constantly implement action plans to improve the balance of all five dimensions of life: work, social (including family), physical, emotional, and spiritual.

GOAL TWO:

MAXIMIZE YOUR COMPANY'S PERFORMANCE

Dynamic Seven

Streamline Your Processes

"The key to defect-free production is a manufacturing process that is (in control)—machinery and equipment well maintained, workplaces clean and orderly, workers well trained, and inspection procedures suited to the rapid detection of deviations."

—David A. Garvin, 1983 McKinsey Award Winner, *Harvard Business Review*[1]

The business of any company is to take specific inputs and transform them through some processes into outputs (the company's products or services).[2] The continued existence and profitability of your company depends on how cost effective you can be as you bring these outputs to market. All the systems, methods, and strategies used to transform inputs into outputs represent the company's *operations*.[3] Ultimately, executives are responsible for operations management, which involves analyzing and implementing all the processes required to transform inputs into outputs.

But, many executives neglect best practices in operations management. Too often, executives do not question or vigorously evaluate business processes. Take, for example, the internal processes involved from the time an order is received to the shipping of that order. Many executives do not even consider how they might streamline such processes to maximize their company's performance.

To increase profits, cut costs, and continue to have a competitive advantage, managers need to effectively streamline their processes.[4] Some business processes can be changed to dramatically improve your bottom line. As your company's leader, you need to be constantly seeking for ways to improve your processes.

In today's business world, it is no longer reasonable to say, "We have been doing things this way forever." The rate at which change is occurring in the business world is faster today then ever before. From this point on, to survive in the climate of rapid change, you should question *every step* in *every operation* to critically determine if any improvements can be made.

Your overall goal should be to remove any waste of time and resources in every process. Consider areas that have been found to waste time and resources in other companies, such as searching activity, transportation procedures, the frequency of product defects, and maintenance.

Try to eliminate activity that does not add value. Shorten your processes to increase your productivity. For example, the printing press should always have ink. Another example: some pizza restaurants have the policy that your pizza will be delivered within 30 minutes or it is free. Any work materials not immediately needed are properly stored to keep a neat, orderly workspace. Such procedures promote greater speed.

Seven common types of wasting of time or resources are (1) overproduction, (2) waiting time, (3) transport of materials, (4) unnecessary work processes, (5) excessive inventory stocks, (6) multiple handling, and (7) defects. Employees should be encouraged to identify any waste of time and resources, and to suggest actions to reduce such waste. At even higher levels of operations management, executives introduce continual improvement processes (CIP) and CIP teams that quickly target and correct process inefficiencies.

Stephen Kline and his wife Bo have come up with a solution to streamlining their processes at Typhoon, a small chain of Thai restaurants that they own and run. They envisioned a handheld computer system to save 15 minutes per table. "They'd be able to place orders more quickly and get notification from the kitchen as soon as dishes were ready," says Kline. The industry norm is a centralized touch-screen computer. Although the new technology is still cutting-edge, Kline believes that the benefits will out weigh the cost.[5]

At the Gold Medal Level, your company keeps a constant lookout for inefficiency in business processes and has implemented self-controlling (Kanban)[6] systems. Development teams and/or specialized consultants focus on the creation of new processes through technological advancements. Thus, there has been a significant decrease in production times.

Regular inspections of employee workstations are made. Your company runs smoothly and efficiently with the latest cost-effective technology. Every employee views himself or herself as being co-responsible for maintaining orderliness and increasing efficiency. By effectively streamlining all areas of operations at this top Gold Medal Level, your company is maximally positioned to respond rapidly to changes in the market, in the economy, and in your competition.

Your business remarkably distinguishes itself from your competitors. As you continually improve your processes and eliminate waste of time or resources, you lower your costs and reduce your delivery times. This creates an added competitive advantage that pleases your customers.

At the top Gold Medal Level, your employees are all motivated to make your company more efficient and effective. You have demonstrated to your customers that you are constantly trying to deliver products and services faster, more efficiently, and more effectively. Your company participates in quality competitions and compares itself with the best. You can celebrate your success and let the local press write about you. Your employees are proud of your business and pleased to be a vital part of your company.

> *"There is less to fear from outside competition than from inside inefficiency...."*
>
> —Author Unknown

Dynamic Seven: Streamline Your Processes		
Score	**Level**	**Description**
☐ 1-5	Endangered Survivor Level	After your company has established its processes, they are not questioned unless problems in the processes arise. Your company places little emphasis on orderliness, and thus your workplace is rather cluttered.
☐ 6-10	Struggling Survivor Level	All work materials that are not needed immediately (such as documents, supplies, files, tools, etc.) are properly stored away. The workplace is kept clean. In the more orderly environment, your employees are more in the mood to suggest further efficiency suggestions. Your employees begin to systematically initiate process improvements.
☐ 11-15	Enduring Survivor Level	The employees of your company have recognized that there is a waste of resources and they have taken action to reduce it. The employees start on their own initiative to standardize their work place. An assigned employee is in charge of monitoring and maintaining orderliness for each work place or department. The company has conducted a "technology audit" to clarify its use and potential needs for technological equipment.

Dynamic Seven: Streamline Your Processes		
Score	**Level**	**Description**
☐ 16-20	Bronze Medal Level	Your company has a continual improvement process (CIP). Any emerging problems are quickly targeted and systematically solved by the work of the CIP teams. CIP teams provide upper management with continuing cost-benefit analyses of emerging technologies that could improve processes. All the needed supplies, tools, files, and documents are kept orderly. Your employees take the initiative to maintain and control cleanness, order, and efficient processes.
☐ 21-25	Silver Medal Level	Every process is systematically monitored and evaluated. When any process has a problem, or is inefficient, or wasting time or resources, then the employees systematically eliminate it. Every employee monitors the seven types of potential waste (overproduction, waiting time, transport, work processes, high inventory stocks, multiple handling, and defects). The increased productivity is measurable. The department and production areas are clean because there are cleaning schedules. Employees can quickly locate equipment, tools, files, and supplies.
☐ 26-30	Gold Medal Level	Regular inspections of employee workstations are made. Your company keeps a constant lookout for inefficiency in business processes and has implemented self-controlling (Kanban) systems. Development teams and/or expert consultants focus on the creation of new processes through technological advancements. Your company runs smoothly and efficiently with the latest cost-effective technology. There has been a significant decrease in production times. Every employee views oneself to be co-responsible for maintaining orderliness and maximizing effectiveness. You are maximally positioned to respond rapidly to changes in the market, in the economy, and in your competition.

Dynamic Eight

Develop Your Suppliers

"Together we'll get better."

—Henri Bergson[1]

Your company cannot directly control everything necessary for its success. When your suppliers provide defective products or deliver their product late, this adversely affects your business. Because your suppliers are an integral part of your business, you need to develop positive business relationships with them.[2] Managing your transactions with suppliers is not a simple matter of buying what is the cheapest. You need to cooperate with your suppliers to negotiate exactly what you need, when you need it, at what quality, and at what price.

But to sustain competitiveness, you need to take the further step of deliberately *developing* your suppliers. You can strengthen your relationships with your suppliers and closely collaborate with them to promptly eliminate any waste of time and resources. You and your suppliers need to create synergies in order to secure your company's future existence in the market. It is precisely because your suppliers are so vitally important for your future existence that you should constantly be developing and improving your relationships with them.

Many executives lead their company to function at the lowest—most primitive—level of relating to suppliers. Thus, they dangerously expose their company to the risk of falling behind its competitors. Such a company restricts its relationships to its suppliers to only the most necessary contacts (such as negotiating price, quality, and delivery dates). These managers tend to be somewhat careless at times in keeping their agreements with suppliers—they figure that they can switch to a competitor of their supplier if that supplier complains about how they are treated.

At this Endangered Survivor Level, a company prefers to produce everything in-house and see suppliers as a "necessary evil" when particular components or supplies need to be purchased from the outside. The general tone of communication with suppliers is not very friendly. Instead, they focus on getting the best deal, behave in a cutthroat and abrupt fashion, "hold their cards" closely, and deliberately conceal their total needs from the supplier.

These business executives treat their suppliers as though they were following the motto, "Disguise and cheat—do not let anyone see our cards." This is a very dangerous and risky game to play. Future success for your company rides on playing with open cards so you can more effectively work together with your suppliers on "win-win" solutions to your needs and to their business. If suppliers do not know exactly what you are trying to accomplish, how will they be able to effectively provide you with exactly what you need?

One of Kmart's suppliers had this scathing remark about dealing with Kmart, "As far as operations, logistics, and so forth, they really suck. As a company, they make commitments and can't stick to them. It's not because of lack of intent; they just can't execute." This vendor sent out a new product line to Kmart stores and it took more than two months for Kmart to display those products, and even then those products were displayed in only 310 out of the 390 stores. This is what the exasperated supplier had to say about the situation, "Some of it got lost, even though we have noticed it was received. Some store managers refused the goods. It's a nightmare doing business with these guys."[3] This supplier's report suggests at least one reason why Kmart has languished at the "endangered survival" level for several years.

Executives who guide their company to rise above this vulnerable, self-defeating stance with suppliers take a number of practical action steps that create a "win-win" relationship with their suppliers. For example, these executives share relevant information about their business operations with their suppliers and provide them with advanced notice of their requirements. This information enables suppliers to custom design and/or plan for on-time delivery of what the company needs. Some of these effective managers design a supplier information sheet to communicate all the specifications that they want their suppliers to fill in the foreseeable future.

At benchmark levels, a company's relationships with its suppliers are strong and the company has few, if any, problems with on-time delivery and quality issues. This is possible because the company's executives and its suppliers have mutually developed a set of goals that specifically lay out what each party wants from each other. And at the same time, you are both continuously working together to find better ways to improve your company's products and processes, as well as your supplier's products and processes.

Once you reach the Gold Medal Level, the employees of your suppliers are "like family" as they collaborate closely with you in your Continuous Improvement Process. Your suppliers' "Kanban" just-in-time delivery system, product quality, and productivity are continually outstanding and improving. Because your suppliers are treated as an integral part of your business that you seek to maintain and strengthen, you have established a reward system for your suppliers' improvements.

At this very top benchmark level, your relationships with your suppliers work smoothly. Top executives integrate their suppliers into their regular strategy day events and meetings. There is an exchange of mutual information for development and improvement. Both you and your suppliers communicate openly and honestly. All operational processes with your suppliers are efficient and effective. Thus, both you and your suppliers benefit from your relationships with one another.

Even when your company reaches this Gold Medal Level, it should not stand still. You should be developing further improved strategies, technologies, and long-term goals for the next couple of years—even up to five years. You should constantly nurture and cultivate your relationships with your suppliers.

> *"For a conscious being, to exist is to change, to change is to mature, to mature is to go on creating oneself endlessly."*
>
> —Henri Bergson[4]

Dynamic Eight: Develop Your Suppliers		
Score	**Level**	**Description**
☐ 1-5	Endangered Survivor Level	The relationship of your company to your suppliers is restricted to only the most necessary contacts (such as discussing quality, delivery dates, and price negotiations). Your company is somewhat careless at times in keeping agreements with suppliers. Company personnel figure they can always switch to competitors of their suppliers if they complain about the actions of your company toward them.
☐ 6-10	Struggling Survivor Level	Your company shares specific information freely with its suppliers so they can more readily serve your needs. Your company and its suppliers are becoming aware of your potentially valuable partnership function, even though you have not yet worked out a close collaborating partnership.
☐ 11-15	Enduring Survivor Level	Your company has narrowed down its suppliers to a few main suppliers with whom you can invest more time in mutual collaboration. Your suppliers collaborate with you in the development and continuous incremental improvement of both your business processes and products.

Dynamic Eight: Develop Your Suppliers		
Score	**Level**	**Description**
☐ 16-20	Bronze Medal Level	Your company has negotiated a set of mutual goals that you would like to accomplish with your suppliers. You are receiving competitive pricing from your suppliers because you stay abreast of pricing trends in their industries. You and your suppliers have a close collaborative relationship because you evaluate and visit your suppliers on a regular basis. You work together on developing and improving your processes and products with the advantage of obtaining advice from your suppliers.
☐ 21-25	Silver Medal Level	Your suppliers function on a "Kanban" just-in-time delivery system in which an automated system provides them daily data on your level of supplies. Thus, your suppliers automatically replenish your supply inventory. You have a computerized, automated supply delivery system that produces competitive advantage for your firm. Your suppliers attend management and technical training programs (such as the 33 Dynamics Seminar) with you to jointly and continually improve their performance and the performance of your company. You regularly throw a "Suppliers Day" party to, thank and celebrate your suppliers for their partnership with your company.
☐ 26-30	Gold Medal Level	The employees of your suppliers are "like family" as they collaborate closely with you in your continuous improvement process. Your suppliers' "Kanban" just-in-time delivery system, product quality, and productivity are continually outstanding and improving. Suppliers are treated as an integral part of your business and you have established a reward system for improvements made by your suppliers.

DYNAMIC NINE

REDUCE YOUR INVENTORY

"If you look at what Dell has done with inventory, we have four days of inventory. Our industry—and Dell specifically—has brought its inventory down much, much faster and much further than most industries."

—MICHAEL DELL, CHAIRMAN, Dell Computers[1]

Many business experts consider an *excessive inventory* to be the most visible symptom of outdated management practices. There are three categories of inventory—raw materials (or component parts), work in process, and finished goods.[2] The executive's goal should be to decrease inventories of all three to the absolute minimum.

In the M.B.A. textbook entitled, *Introduction to Managerial Accounting*, Professors Folk, Garrison, and Noreen ask this penetrating question, "Why do excessive inventories result from the desire to maximize production and to keep everyone busy and why are they a problem?"[3]

Many companies are blissfully mesmerized with the enticing notion that "maintaining a large inventory is necessary to provide fast, 100% delivery of its products."[4] But this is not always true! Many executives are quite surprised to learn that, in reality, many of the businesses with the shortest delivery times are the ones that have the smallest inventories.

Some companies hold large inventories as "insurance" in case anything unexpected happens, such as a supplier's late or defective delivery or the receipt of an unanticipated large order by a customer. Although there can be some advantages to storing large inventory in some industries, it is not without a significant cost. Companies holding significant inventories tie up large amounts of their available capital in materials, work in process, and finished goods. Further, they incur the added costs to store this vast inventory, and suffer the additional labor costs and/or inefficiency associated with having to handle a larger flow of product tracking information and materials.

But that is not all. There's even more to the "down side" of the story of excessive inventories.

The policy of holding large inventories greatly reduces manager and employee motivation for honing their skills to produce near defect-free products with great efficiency and effectiveness. Why? Because the large inventory "insulates" them from the need to do so. The company with a large stock of inventory tends to cover up and even fail to detect many of their process problems, inefficiencies, and waste. Holding large inventories thereby tends to produce sloppy and inefficient work. Managers and employees become less flexible and less innovative in designing performance improvements. This, in turn, causes greater waste of time and resources, and a higher frequency of defects.

So the high cost of large inventories tends to significantly undermine the level of efficiency in operations, further hindering the company from reaching its potential level of profitability.

For example, if you store large inventories of partially finished products, you can run into many problems such as defects from previous workstations going unnoticed due to the long periods of time between workstations. Further, if a machine is not calibrated properly or defects are being caused by employee failure to follow procedures properly, such problems will not be promptly detected or easily traced back to their source if your company stores large work-in-process inventories. Once you decide to deliberately reduce your inventory, any concealed waste, inefficiencies, and hidden problems will tend to surface and can be promptly eradicated.

One final problem can be noted: Companies accumulating large inventories of finished goods run the risk that those products may become out of date or obsolete.[5]

Dell Computers are assembled promptly upon receipt of each individual order. Only a very minimal inventory is kept of components or work-in-process products. Factories are located close to suppliers who deliver parts as needed. With the rapid technological advances in computer components, keeping a large inventory of finished computers would risk obsolescence of the inventory. Dell rapidly rose to the top of the computer manufacturing companies by its innovative operations that eliminated the need to maintain a large inventory.

For some industries—such as the manufacturers of flu vaccine, Halloween costumes, or Christmas cards—current technology for production may require short-term stockpiling of the seasonal product to have it ready for massive shipments to customers all at one time on the calendar when it is in demand. But even with flu vaccine, it does not make good business sense to produce an excessive inventory, because the specific vaccine that is produced is only effective for the current year. Any excess inventory that is unsold must be destroyed, because next year's vaccine will be different—depending on the results of scientific research on the strain of flu being spread that particular year.

So, although there may be specific exceptions for certain industries, in general if a company wants to maximize its overall performance, it is a good idea to cut back on its inventory. Reducing your inventory frees up capital, can give your company greater flexibility, reduce defects, and reduce costs—all of which helps your company run more efficiently and effectively. Even in industries where carrying an inventory is necessary, the goal should be to maintain only the minimum sufficient inventory. This will maximize profitability.

It is essential that your decision to reduce your product inventory be linked with making the types of performance improvements that are discussed in:

- ❖Dynamic 7—Streamline Your Processes,
- ❖Dynamic 8—Develop Your Suppliers, and
- ❖Dynamic 32—Increase Your Delivery Performance.

As you develop toward benchmark levels for these dynamics, you will be much better positioned to maintain small inventories in order to maximize your performance, become more efficient, effective, and profitable. With a small inventory, your company will be able to reduce your process time, speed up the flow of information and documents, and increase your delivery performance to your customers.

Reaching the Gold Medal Level will require that your company develop an effective *just-in-time* (JIT) system. Just-in-time means that raw materials or component parts are received "just in time" when needed and that products are manufactured right when they are needed for delivery to customers. This enables your company to run so efficiently and effectively that you will need little to no inventory. Thus, the costs associated with holding a large inventory have been eliminated.

Companies—such as Dell—have massively reduced their inventory by implementing just-in-time supply chain systems. By contrast, the Apple computer manufacturer has struggled with excessively large inventories. Even though they have been working on this money-draining problem, they have suffered its effects, becoming less competitive than Dell. A smaller inventory level is a challenge to reach even for Fortune 500 companies such as Dell, but working toward this goal can substantially help companies compete and sustain significant competitive advantages.

In some industries, some companies will never be able to reach this "just-in-time" level. For other companies it may take several years, if not decades, to achieve the "just-in-time" standard. But in any event the closer a company can get to this standard, the greater its competitive potential.

There have been many companies large and small who have implemented the JIT approach with great success. Here is a list of a few: Black and Decker, Borg-Warner, Bose, Goodyear, General Motors, Ford

Motor Company, Intel, John Deere, Tektronix, and Westinghouse. These companies—and thousands more—have reaped significant competitive benefits of implementing a JIT system:

1. Capital that had been tied up in inventory can now be used more strategically.
2. Delivery performance is increased.
3. Storage space can be eliminated or used in more productive way than storing inventory.
4. Defects are more rapidly detected and reduced, which results in lower costs and higher customer satisfaction.[6]

After implementing lean manufacturing that has helped them streamline their processes, Numonics Corporation, a manufacturer of communication devices, can now produce and ship products on the same day. Being able to streamline their processes has allowed Numonics to reduce their inventory from $1.5 million to $800,000. They have also been able to cut production space by 8,000 square feet and increase their annual inventory turns from 5.5 to 9. Even when the manufacturing industry is in a down turn, Numonics remains profitable, in large part due to these highly cost-effective process improvements.

"If it weren't for lean, I don't even like to think where we'd be," plant manager Pat Burns says. "We'd be in the red, and our inventory would be through the roof." The wise management decisions by Burns to seek out professional consultation to implement lean manufacturing enabled Numonics to stay afloat in a recession.[7] Thus, achieving the benchmark of a greatly reduced inventory not only has the potential to increase your profitability, but can literally preserve your company's very existence during serious economic down turns.

"Inventory is evil!"

—Dr. Ron Snyder, university business professor, & former executive in Fortune 500 companies

Dynamic Nine: Reduce Your Inventory		
Score	Level	Description
☐ 1-5	Endangered Survivor Level	There are excessive stocks of inventory of most of the products of your company. Your company does not know where its process problems are because, in part, it carries large raw materials, work in process, and finished goods inventories.
☐ 6-10	Struggling Survivor Level	Your company has recognized its inventory problem. And your company is working on reducing its product inventory, work in process, and/or raw materials inventories, getting rid of old inventory, and better organizing its remaining inventory.
☐ 11-15	Enduring Survivor Level	Your employees understand the benefits of reducing inventories. Your company is reducing product inventory, decreasing the excess quantity of goods received by suppliers, and increasing the frequency of smaller deliveries from suppliers scheduled to arrive when needed. As a result, you have been able to reduce your inventory storage space and costs. Your annual inventory turnover rate has been increased.

Dynamic Nine: Reduce Your Inventory		
Score	**Level**	**Description**
☐ 16-20	Bronze Medal Level	With the participation of employees, your company has developed clear goals for further reducing inventory and has put controls in place to prevent overstocking. Your suppliers are involved in actively reducing your raw materials inventory.
☐ 21-25	Silver Medal Level	Both your employees and suppliers are involved in your company-wide automatic control system (Kanban control system) for inventory management.
☐ 26-30	Gold Medal Level	Your company has achieved a highly effective just-in-time system. Your company runs so efficiently and effectively that there is little to no accumulated inventory. Materials arrive and products are shipped out just in time. The costs associated with holding a large inventory have been eliminated.

Dynamic Ten

Measure Work Efficiency

"You never know a line is crooked unless you have a straight one to put next to it."

—Socrates

Numonics Corporation, which manufacturers communication devices such as digital whiteboards, was having some problems with an electronic pen that it was manufacturing for a computer peripheral. Pat Burns, the plant manager, turned to Rich Stewart and Keith Ashlock from the Delaware Valley Industrial Resource Center (DVIRC) for help.

Although the pen was superior to its predecessor, it was taking longer to manufacture and more defects were occurring. Ashlock and Stewart went to work immediately and began to have a series of training sessions for the employees on lean manufacturing methodology. "The company had never invested in this kind of training before, and it was totally new to them," says Burns. Burns and his employees were led through a "kaizen blitz," where they broke down their manufacturing process on paper and redesigned the manufacturing process into work cells. Then they put their new design to work by moving the machinery to more efficient locations for running the new manufacturing process.

What impressed Burns was that once the system was finished, "it was the employee's system." This was not a system that was unilaterally installed by management. It took three months before everything was up and running for Numonics Corporation, but there were dramatic improvements just in two weeks. The time it took to produce one pen fell from around 50 minutes to 17 minutes. The previous system's failure rate was 45 percent and the new system produced only 1.2 percent defects. Burns says that the training in lean manufacturing helped him analyze every aspect of production. "We broke down and found out that the biggest failures were due to PC boards, a component that we don't manufacture," Burns explained. "We went back to the vendor, and they corrected the problem."[1]

"Do more faster with fewer resources." If this is humanly possible, it can only be done by increasing efficiency and productivity levels.[2] When you continually increase your efficiency and productivity, your company is literally able to "do more faster and with fewer resources," as the Numonics Corporation did.

Of course, it is not fair to assign more work to employees than they can realistically achieve. But even the most dedicated employees can be surprised by the significant increases in their work efficiency that occurs when their work is measured and visualized on charts on a daily basis. One important key is to encourage your employees to become actively involved in increasing their own productivity, and in increasing the overall productivity of the business processes.

Measuring your employees' work efficiency is essential to maximize your company's performance. To do so meaningfully, you must compare each individual's performance to a specific set of pertinent standards.[3] Standards provide the necessary reference points that enable you to determine whether the observed data on employee performance is below, matches, or exceeds the standards. Without carefully crafted standards as the basis for your evaluation, it is impossible to realistically and objectively measure your employee's work efficiency. So it boils down to this: Your company's competitive capacity depends on setting excellent, high, yet achievable standards for each employee.

Effectiveness is doing the right thing. Efficiency is doing things the right way with the minimum use of time and resources to get the job done properly. In order to do the right thing, you must know what it is. In order to do things the right way, you must first know what the right way is. These are your standards when you state them in quantitative, measurable terms.

To be fair to your employees, and to obtain the level of work performance from them that you desire, you will need to communicate your standards of effectiveness and efficiency to each employee. This should be done well in advance of the time you measure how well they adhere to those standards.

Your company should strive to increase its efficiency each and every year. The only way you can do this is by collecting the appropriate data, facts, and figures on how each individual employee is performing. Then you will be able to set specific, higher achievable goals each year and thus finally realize those goals. This process of carefully measuring your employees' work efficiency can increase your company's overall productivity and profits.

At the Gold Medal Level, executives set efficiency goals for every business level in the company and the company steadily achieves higher and higher levels of efficiency. Employees, too, are actively involved in submitting improvement proposals for process efficiency, and they progressively increase their own efficiency levels by refining their own process steps. Furthermore, every department evaluates every other department, resulting in new ideas that lead to innovative process improvements.

At this very high level, employees—as well as departments—consistently achieve their high goals in efficiency. The company continually evaluates and develops its efficiency standards. As new technologies become available, you make sure that your standards are immediately adjusted accordingly. Your reward systems are periodically updated with higher standards as the company increases its efficiency and productivity.

> *"I always arrive late at the office, but I make up for it by leaving early."*
>
> —Charles Lamb

Dynamic Ten: Measure Work Efficiency		
Score	**Level**	**Description**
☐ 1-5	Endangered Survivor Level	Your company does not measure the work efficiency of your employees. Management alone sets the production and/or service goals.
☐ 6-10	Struggling Survivor Level	The employees of your company work on orders as they are received. They follow production plans and pursue production and/or service goals of management. However, efficiency standards are in the process of being developed for future implementation.
☐ 11-15	Enduring Survivor Level	Your company has developed a set of efficiency standards and is routinely measuring the work efficiency of each employee based on those standards.

Dynamic Ten: Measure Work Efficiency		
Score	**Level**	**Description**
☐ 16-20	Bronze Medal Level	Your company is finding new ways of increasing work efficiency, making it possible to progressively upgrade its efficiency standards. Employees collaborate in setting individual, production, and departmental goals to increase efficiency.
☐ 21-25	Silver Medal Level	Your company has measurable goals for improving efficiency and is continually improving its processes. A motivational system is in place that meaningfully rewards and commends employees who meet or exceed efficiency standards.
☐ 26-30	Gold Medal Level	Efficiency goals are set for every business level in your company. The company steadily achieves higher and higher levels of efficiency. Employees are actively involved in submitting improvement proposals for process efficiency. Employees progressively increase their own efficiency levels by refining their own process steps. Every department evaluates every other department, resulting in new innovative process improvements.

Dynamic Eleven

Manage Information Effectively

"If a piece of information is not used, it is a liability, not an asset."

—Bernard Liautaud, CEO of Business Objects[1]

We are in the information age. Countless quantities of information lie at our fingertips. If we could only harness this information, we would be able to solve many more of our business problems.

H. G. Wells observed,

> "An immense and ever-increasing wealth of knowledge is scattered about the world today; knowledge that would probably suffice to solve all the mighty difficulties of our age, but it is dispersed and unorganized. We need a sort of mental clearinghouse for the mind: a depot where knowledge and ideas are received, sorted, summarized, digested, clarified and compared."[2]

Your company needs an Information Technology (IT) system to serve as that "mental clearinghouse" to help you manage your information effectively.

Solectron, a company that manufactures cell phones, computer devices, and memory chips, realized the need for implementing a state-of-the-art IT system to manage information effectively. Solectron decided to outsource their IT operations to IBM in order to free up their own time and resources. Although they have outsourced their IT operations, Solectron makes sure that each of their employees has a basic knowledge about how the system effects their own department. An executive with Solectron, Bernard Mathaisel, explained, "We're going to have to build knowledge communities with military precision, beginning with a skills assessment of every person in the company, followed by instructor-led training and online courseware." By outsourcing the IT function, Solectron executives believe that they will be able to focus on *using* the information from the system.[3]

The ability to manage information effectively helps your company strategically position itself in your industry. A fine-tuned information system can serve as a valuable tool. It can equip executives to recognize and take action on strategic opportunities such as:

- further developing existing products,
- creating barriers to entry by potential competitors,
- changing the basis of competition,
- changing the balance of supply relationships, and
- changing organizational objectives.

Additional benefits occur in operations, such as:

- increasing efficiency,
- reducing costs,
- increasing delivery speed,
- reducing excessive clerical work,
- creating greater flexibility,
- providing information on a more timely basis,
- making decisions on real-time data,
- achieving better insight into product development, and
- facilitating much better harmonization.

To stay competitive in your industry, your company must manage its information effectively.

Walgreens innovated a great way to do this. This drug store chain's information system makes it possible to walk into any Walgreens store and get your prescription filled, because each store is linked to a central system that can be accessed by any Walgreens store. Walgreens has risen to the Gold Medal Level in that its information system has become one of its most powerful competitive advantages.[4]

At the Gold Medal Level, a company effectively uses its information system throughout the entire company. The right information is delivered in the most convenient, user-friendly way to the right people at the right time. If the information system is not considered part of the company's core competence, then the Management Information Systems (MIS) and Information Technology (IT) operations are outsourced for maximal effectiveness.

Solectron Corporation outsourced their IT function to IBM's Global Services for more than 50 facilities and subsidiaries. The 10-year contract was one of the largest ever awarded to a service company at $1.8 billion.

Corporate Vice President, Bernard Mathaisel said that Solectron had little choice but to rely on outside IT help: With an annual growth rate of 50 percent and revenue expected to reach more than $20 billion in fiscal year 2001, outsourcing was a necessity. "In a world of limited talent resources, there was no way to sustain both our rapid business growth and support our diverse IT operations," he explained.

Many companies such as Cisco, Household Finance, and Avon have outsourced their IT function and are using real-time data analysis tools from Verilytics. Verilytics helps these companies take real time information and make it useful to decision-makers within the company.

In 1971, Louis and Tom Borders started a bookstore they called Borders. The brothers wanted to offer a larger variety of books in their store and knew that the only way they could do this would be if they could turn inventory more quickly. So the brothers created an inventory-tracking system that made it easy for the salesclerks to find out what was on the shelves and what was on order. This management information system was so effective that the company started selling it to other bookstores and this became their primary business. It was only later that they opened more bookstores all over the country.[5]

At the Gold Medal Level, the company's information system is fine-tuned and effectively manages information that is useful for decision-making. Not only is the relevant information delivered to the right users at the right time, but also it is delivered in the most convenient way possible. This requires regular communication among your employees who share relevant information openly across departments.

> *"Knowledge will create wealth. Our primary goal will be to make the knowledge productive."*
>
> —Peter Drucker[6]

Dynamic Eleven: Manage Information Effectively		
Score	**Level**	**Description**
☐ 1-5	Endangered Survivor Level	Whether an information system exists in your company or not, no one is managing the information.
☐ 6-10	Struggling Survivor Level	Your company has a hard time accessing information that you realize you need for managerial decision-making. Although you may have analyzed the opportunities and costs of implementing an Information Technology (IT) system, information is still unsystematically gathered at your company. Therefore information is not used effectively during the decision-making process.
☐ 11-15	Enduring Survivor Level	Your company uses information for decision-making only at the operational level. It is difficult for your company to get relevant information to the right users.

Dynamic Eleven: Manage Information Effectively		
Score	**Level**	**Description**
☐ 16-20	Bronze Medal Level	Your company uses information from your IT function to make decisions at your operational, tactical, and strategic levels.
☐ 21-25	Silver Medal Level	Your information system has been analyzed and modified to collect information that is useful for decision-making. That information is then delivered in a timely manner to the people who need it for decision-making. Occasional information overloads or bottlenecks may occur.
☐ 26-30	Gold Medal Level	Your company effectively uses its information system throughout the entire company. The right information is delivered in the most convenient, user-friendly way to the right people at the right time. If the information system is not considered part of the core competence of the company, then the Management Information Systems (MIS) and Information Technology (IT) operations are outsourced for maximal effectiveness.

Dynamic Twelve

Monitor Through Controls

"The essence of mathematics is not to make simple things complicated, but to make complicated things simple."

—S. Gudder[1]

Like every other weekday, Emily Coker, 45, got to work early to brew a fresh pot of coffee and read the daily paper before beginning work. She was a bookkeeper for a small-sized New York City law firm. But this particular morning, Coker had a tough time enjoying her cup of coffee and had quite a bit of trouble focusing on reading the newspaper because she was worrying about her recent credit card statement for her Christmas gift spending. She hadn't realized that her spending had exceeded her credit limit, and she didn't have enough money to cover the minimum required payment by the due date.

Finally, Coker felt relieved when it occurred to her that she could easily take a small "loan" from either the company's cash reserves or trust funds because she had control over all the bookkeeping and had access to the company's bank accounts. Coker selected one of the firm's trust accounts that she thought would be least detectable. Then she rationalized her unorthodox decision by thinking, "If I can just borrow enough money to make this payment, I can keep from ruining my credit rating. Then I can easily return the money when my paycheck comes in. No one will ever know or really be harmed by this little 'loan' that I urgently need."

Payday rolled around, but Coker put off repaying the money she had "borrowed" due to other unanticipated household bills. Because it was so convenient, soon Coker began "borrowing" more and more money from the firm's accounts. Nothing happened. Nothing stood in her way.

Eventually, Coker was "borrowing" hundreds and even thousands of dollars per week. One day when Coker was on vacation, one of the law firm partners urgently had to write a substantial check on a client's trust account, but a few days later, he was notified that the check "bounced." Calling the bank, the law partner was told that there was an insufficient balance, due to a series of increasingly large checks that had been drawn against that account in recent months. He promptly informed his partner and the two of them went down to the bank where they discovered that Coker had taken an estimated $375,000 from a number of their trust and cash accounts over a three-year period.

Financial fraud is not restricted to the giant corporations such as Enron and WorldCom in the USA, Parmalat in Italy or the retail giant Ahold in the Netherlands. Corporations of all sizes have suffered losses and even bankruptcy due to corrupt practices by employees. Recent news of financial scandals and fraud in the corporate world has served to mightily underscore the vital responsibility of company executives to establish and maintain adequate financial controls. But monitoring through controls is not simply for the purpose of avoiding a financial scandal. And monitoring is not designed to make simple things more complicated than they are.

Instead, there is a highly useful side to monitoring that, in a sense, "simplifies" the work of the executive. On the positive side is this key observation: Every top-performing executive who manages with consistent excellence over the long haul is known to be highly effective in:

1. protecting company assets,
2. obtaining accurate and reliable accounting records and information for timely and successful managerial decision-making,
3. ensuring efficient operations, and
4. measuring compliance to management's policies and procedures.

What is the management tool that makes all this possible? Highly successful companies employ a carefully crafted *internal control system* that provides the specific procedures, practices, and policies needed to accomplish these four highly essential objectives.

In the current, increasingly strict legal environment for corporations in the United States, many experienced business leaders have become reluctant to serve on the board of directors of other companies. Why? Because they fear being held liable should that company turn out to have the all too common problem of an inadequate internal control system.

In the absence of adequate internal controls, unacceptable risks and exposures occur. "Exposures" are weaknesses in the internal control system, which lead to various kinds of dangerous risks:

- ❖theft of company assets,
- ❖destruction of assets,
- ❖corrupt information, and
- ❖disruption in the system.

No board member or executive wants any of these outcomes to occur on his or her watch! It seems that nearly every week, the news media broadcasts the pictures of yet another shamed business leader caught in the tangled web of financial mismanagement or outright scandalous fraud. Thankfully, the world's best executives implement the necessary management controls and high ethical standards to avoid such a humiliating outcome.

So what specific controls are available to prevent the drastic consequences of mismanagement or financial scandal? Highly effective executives rely upon three levels of controls:

- ❖preventive controls,
- ❖detective controls, and
- ❖corrective controls.

Preventive controls are what you could call the "first line of defense." Preventive controls substantially (but not completely) reduce the occurrence of undesirable events. A preventive control will force compliance with a prescribed action and thus act like a "screen" that effectively blocks out many potential bad events.

Detective controls deal with problems that get through the "screen" of your preventive controls. Detective controls involve techniques, devices, or procedures that identify undesirable events that get through the first line of defense. Thus, they could be seen as the "second line of defense." The detective controls sound an alarm when a problem happens or when there is a departure from an established standard.

Corrective controls are the "last line of defense." When a problem gets detected, the corrective controls should take action. There is a big difference between detective controls and corrective controls. Detective controls identify and alert while corrective controls actually fix the problem.[2]

Although no system of internal controls is perfect, executives should carefully weigh the cost to improve controls in relation to the added benefits of that improvement.

In addition to using preventive, detective, and corrective controls, top executives also use *financial ratios* to monitor and control business functions. For example, some financial ratios commonly used by executives are:

- ❖Return on Assets (ROA),
- ❖Return on Equity (ROE),
- ❖Profit Margin (Net Income/Sales),
- ❖Inventory Turnover Ratio (Cost of Goods Sold/ Average Inventories),
- ❖Debt to Equity Ratio, and
- ❖Current Ratio (Current Assets/Current Liabilities).

Financial ratios reflect what is actually going on in the company and point in the direction of what really needs to be managed. Because finance is the basic language of business, top executives find that regularly calculating various financial ratios is vitally important for their managerial decision-making.

Ratios guide management in making successful decisions for the long run while also helping guide effective short-term decisions. In a business world where the business climate can change day-by-day, ratios help narrow down the most important issues that need management's immediate attention.

Ratios show a connection that exists between different parts of the business. Knowing the main ratios allows management to work with different departments on the overall business objectives of the organization.

Successful executive management that succeeds over the long haul requires that its plans be implemented in a business setting that has strong control systems. This is the only way to insure that the managers' plans are actually implemented properly and then adjusted over time to respond to unanticipated developments. In his book, *You Can Start a Business*, Laurence Holt provides the explanations of a general manager and a financial manager on how they routinely monitor through controls:

> *General Manager:* "My role within the company is the efficient use of resources, money, and manpower to maximize the output within the factory. We operate a very horizontal structure with a number of key areas that determine the level of output we are achieving. By monitoring those areas I can get a very clear view of what is happening on an almost daily basis. Sales is important and I need to know from our sales people what they are anticipating during the month or longer and from there to organize the resources within the factory to meet those orders or anticipated orders."
>
> *Financial Manager:* "Each month we do a financial report on profit and loss and cash flow and balance sheet. This month we have been looking at the profit and loss. I have been discussing with the general manager the

> various differences there have been concerning our actual achievements and what we had in the budget. One of the areas that came to our attention was the stock. We looked at work in process and finished goods, which ended up higher than in the budget. We discussed the matter and the general manager explained that he had built for sales, which weren't actually achieved, and this increased the work in progress and finished goods at the end of the month. We also looked at the materials purchased during the month, which were lower than forecasted. The reason for this was that they had built product in the previous month and had not had to buy so much material for the current month. When we looked over the year as a whole we were very much on target."[3]

In companies that reach the Gold Medal Level, effective and comprehensive controls are in place at all levels of the organization. These firms use a customized benchmark system of financial analysis. At every level of the organization, adequate controls are in place, helping to assure the fulfillment of management's objectives. Further, the company's financial data is regularly benchmarked against the performance of the leading firms of the industry.

A principle stated for agricultural business in an ancient proverb certainly applies to all forms of business generally:

> *"Be sure you know the condition of your flocks, give careful attention to your herds..."*[4]

Dynamic Twelve: Monitor Through Controls		
Score	**Level**	**Description**
☐ 1-5	Endangered Survivor Level	No controls are in place, and the company has no system for using financial data for managerial control.
☐ 6-10	Struggling Survivor Level	A few controls are in place, but there is still no use of financial analysis tools.
☐ 11-15	Enduring Survivor Level	There are some sets of controls in place that help monitor the employees. There is limited use of financial analysis to monitor and control business functions.

Dynamic Twelve: Monitor Through Controls		
Score	**Level**	**Description**
☐ 16-20	Bronze Medal Level	There are basic sets of controls in place that help monitor the employees. All the basic financial ratios are calculated and used in managerial monitoring and control.
☐ 21-25	Silver Medal Level	There are adequate internal controls in place throughout the organization. Detective and corrective controls are in place. Financial ratios are calculated and compared to previous years to monitor and control company functions.
☐ 26-30	Gold Medal Level	An effective and comprehensive internal control system is in place covering all levels of the organization. Preventive, detective, and corrective controls are effectively used. Your company uses a customized benchmark system of financial analysis, including ongoing use of financial ratios in managerial monitoring, control, and other decision-making.

GOAL THREE:

DEVELOP A SUPERIOR WORKFORCE

Dynamic Thirteen

Select an Excellent Workforce

"I believe that the most important dynamic in all of business is an excellent workforce. Managers must remember that their number one asset is their human resources. Find the best people in the industry and your company will soar!"
—Sam Johnston, Founder and CEO, Johnston Avionics

A survey of the most successful companies revealed that hiring employees is one of the most challenging aspects of growth. When a company is growing fast, you have less time to make sure that you are hiring the best workforce.

"When you're fast growing, you don't take as much care with hiring as you should," confesses Ross Youngs, the CEO of Unicenture, a company that produces CD storage products located in Columbus,

Ohio. But Young learned that carelessness in hiring doesn't pay in the long run: "Now we don't take gambles. We have multiple eyes on any major candidate."[1]

Many small- and medium-sized businesses have the continuing problem of not being able to find enough qualified candidates to hire. For many open positions, there is a lack of high quality, skilled, competent personnel with the characteristics that small- and medium-sized companies need. Selecting the right workforce is very important, but it takes time to recruit and hire the right people for the job.

Dan Weinfurter, founder of Parson Group, contends, "You have to grow quickly, or others will beat you at your game."[2] But because it takes time to find the best personnel, rushing this process can jeopardize the quality of the employees that you hire. That is why Parson Group didn't open offices in the major cities with the largest market potential because the right kind of employees were not available in those cites. Instead they opened offices in the locations where they knew they could find the best employees to manage their offices. These high quality employees are sometimes called "A" employees.

Here are some questions that the astute executive should answer:

- What are the key characteristics of the best employees for each of our positions?
- Are there ways to distinguish between the right person and the wrong person for my particular business?
- Where can I find the best personnel?
- How can I select the best person from all the applicants?

To be successful, you must hire the best applicants in your industry. Someone who went a step further was Dharmesh Shah, one of the founders of Pyramid Digital Solutions Inc. In 1994, Shah started his business in Birmingham, Alabama, because that is where he had worked for U.S. Steel Group. Shah soon found out that "there's not a lot of technology talent in Birmingham."[3] Shah realized that he needed to move his company to some other region in the country because of the lack of qualified personnel in Birmingham. One of his employees was a highly specialized programmer who lived in Chicago and commuted between Chicago and Birmingham. But when he became a father, commuting became a problem. The only way Shah could keep this "A" employee would be to open an office in Chicago. That is exactly what he ended up doing.

Shah is committed to what he calls the "follow-the-talent policy." Shah conducts business where the talent is. He currently employs 27 people in Boston, 21 in Birmingham, 9 in Chicago, and he is opening an office in New York City with 2 additional employees. "Since we've already made the logistical leap to four places, we'll probably expand more." The only downside to this policy, Shah admits, is the lack of a unified "small-company atmosphere." Nonetheless, he believes that each location makes up for this disadvantage by having its own identity.[4]

Shah's management practice clearly adds significant value to his company. An Intel executive quoted by Walter Kiechell, III, emphasized the importance of managerial contributions to the human resource demands of a thriving company, "Even as a manager, you have to add value. You have to be good at something in the arena you're working in. You can't just say, 'Well, I am a manager so I will just manage and coordinate these people.' People don't require that kind of management anymore."[5]

Companies that reach the Gold Medal Level hire and retain the best applicants. They carefully consider the personality characteristics required for performing the tasks of a given position in order to hire the right candidate for the job.

The optimal recruitment of personnel for your business environment is not just one more dynamic among many. It is one of the most important dynamics for business success. Your ultimate executive concern should be to recruit, meet the needs of, and retain excellent employees. Hiring the best employees and correctly positioning them in the right job maximizes your employees' performance and thereby enhances your company's productivity.

> *"You want an excited workforce, a workforce where every individual is daily adding value towards the business strategy."*
>
> —James Fitzpatrick, President, Navtech Inc.

Dynamic Thirteen: Select an Excellent Workforce		
Score	**Level**	**Description**
☐ 1-5	Endangered Survivor Level	Whoever is available for a designated position is hired. A comprehensive method for employee selection does not exist.
☐ 6-10	Struggling Survivor Level	Employees are selected by using criteria that are incomplete or inappropriate (i.e., acceptable wage, a salary) and there is no clearly defined job description.
☐ 11-15	Enduring Survivor Level	Employees are selected according to task descriptions and the job requirements of the position.

Dynamic Thirteen: Select an Excellent Workforce		
Score	Level	Description
☐ 16-20	Bronze Medal Level	Assessment tools are used to carefully select applicants that match task descriptions and job requirements.
☐ 21-25	Silver Medal Level	Not only does your company hire the best applicants available, but they are also the best applicants in the industry.
☐ 26-30	Gold Medal Level	Not only does the company hire and retain the best applicants, but management also carefully matches personality characteristics of applicants to the job tasks in order to hire the right candidate for the position.

Dynamic Fourteen

Communicate Openly

"It means integrity; it means other people can trust you...it means you don't have a hidden agenda; that you're straightforward and when you say something you mean it; that you can be believed. Imagine trying to run a company if people didn't believe you. Just imagine."

—Jack Bogle[1]

Every employee should be fully informed about anything that has to do with his or her work. Open communication doesn't mean that you tell every employee absolutely everything. Exhaustive communication would just be too time-consuming, chaotic, (and you guessed it) exhausting! But open, appropriate and truthful communication is necessary for coordinating and motivating your employees to work at the highest level of productivity.

Ken Blanchard, the successful author of *The One Minute-Manager*, compares business with a bowling alley. The employee takes a bowling ball in his hand and has to clear all 10 pins, if possible. But imagine that instead of a normal bowling lane where he can see the bowling pins, there is a curtain between the employee and the bowling pins. The ball passes under the curtain, the employee hears the falling of some bowling pins, but never learns the full result. He or she only gets delayed feedback and usually only when something goes wrong.

Open communication is like removing the curtain. Results are conveyed immediately, and no crucial information is withheld. Our favorite book, the Bible, has a passage that describes the advantage of openness, expressed in terms of "light":

> "Live as children of light (for the fruit of the light consists in all goodness, righteousness and truth).... For it is shameful even to mention what the disobedient do in secret. But everything exposed by the light becomes visible, for it is the light that makes everything visible."[2]

It is difficult for some people to communicate openly with fellow employees who may be different from them in age, race, gender, religion, or sub-culture. Managers can overcome mistrust, tension, stereotyping, and communication problems associated with diversity in the workplace by a number of educational, managerial, and interpersonal approaches. Jesus said, "So in everything, do to others what you would have them do to you...."[3] This is very practical advice.

Diversity training programs have been developed by over half of all organizations in the United States to help employees identify their stereotypic biases, to improve acceptance, to reduce mistrust, and to develop interpersonal skills to overcome communication difficulties.[4] These diversity-training programs include the components of building awareness and skills. Increasing awareness helps employees to be sensitized to the automatic assumptions they may make about others, and how these assumptions affect their communication, judgment, decision-making, and work behavior. In this way, the stereotypical myths of cultural subgroups are overcome. Skill building helps both managers and employees to acquire skills to communicate effectively with co-workers and customers from other sub-cultural groups.

Also, managers can model good attitudes and appropriate communication with employees and customers of diverse backgrounds. Company policies can be formulated and discussed to hold employees accountable to treat one another openly with equal respect, dignity, and value. For example, company policies and corporate culture can promote tolerance and acceptance of diversity in the workforce. Transformational leadership[5] can make a major contribution in this context. Thus, there are policy improvements, group interventions, educational training, and one-to-one methods to overcome the obstacles of diversity in the workplace that may interfere with open and effective communication.

With a climate of open communication, employees are encouraged to share openly what is on their mind and respectfully "tell it how it is." Employees feel more free to tell the truth if they are allowed the opportunity. Hypocrisy becomes less likely when employees are allowed to openly state what they think.

Holding back information that the employee needs will only breed mistrust in the workplace. When there is mistrust, there is the perception that the employer is lying to the employees. Managers sometimes conceal information pertinent to an employee's job in order to deceive the employee in some way. A Hebrew proverb gives some very helpful advice at this point. It says, "...the tongue of the wise brings healing. Truthful lips endure forever, but a lying tongue lasts only a moment."[6] Another teaching from an ancient book of wisdom advises us, "...each of you must put off falsehood and speak truthfully to his neighbor...."[7]

At the Gold Medal Level, the company maintains continuous, transparent communication. The environment and means are provided by managers so that each employee is encouraged to share openly.

Top companies achieve the vision of continuous "real time" open communication. Dan Bollom, CEO of Wisconsin Public Service, remarked, "Vision is what you want to become. Everyone must know where you want the organization to go or you will never get there."[8]

Having total communication allows for a positive work environment where each problem is appropriately addressed and dealt with in a timely and effective manner. Honesty and sincerity become a continual reality in the business. Employees feel free to express themselves and are encouraged to openly state what they think without feeling threatened by anyone. This can keep employees more motivated and productive because they not only feel better understood, but they also feel like they are truly "in the loop."

Ralph Waldo Emerson once said, "It is a luxury to be understood."[9] At the Gold Medal Level, your company enjoys this luxury.

> *"Honesty is the first chapter in the book of wisdom."*
> —THOMAS JEFFERSON

Dynamic Fourteen: Communicate Openly		
Score	**Level**	**Description**
☐ 1-5	Endangered Survivor Level	Managers conceal most information from employees. There is poor and sometimes even misleading communication in the company resulting in mistrust and rumors.
☐ 6-10	Struggling Survivor Level	Only a select few employees receive adequate company information.
☐ 11-15	Enduring Survivor Level	Managers communicate "need to know" information to key employees, and communicate only the information that is legally required to all other employees.

Dynamic Fourteen: Communicate Openly		
Score	**Level**	**Description**
☐ 16-20	Bronze Medal Level	All employees are periodically informed about company developments through regular publications and company meetings.
☐ 21-25	Silver Medal Level	Employees are kept fully informed continuously about every relevant aspect of the company.
☐ 26-30	Gold Medal Level	The company maintains total open communication. Managers create the environment and the means for each employee to share openly. The company atmosphere is one of mutual trust and support.

Dynamic Fifteen

Motivate Your Workforce

"I have never seen a man who could do real work except under the stimulus of encouragement and the approval of the people for whom he is working."

—Charles Schwab[1]

A Lou Harris poll reported some startling findings:

- ❖63 percent of American workers believed that people don't work as hard as people did 10 years ago.
- ❖78 percent of American workers believe that people take less pride in their work.
- ❖69 percent of American workers believe that overall workmanship is substandard.
- ❖73 percent of American workers believe that workers are less motivated.[2]

These data pose a serious challenge for American executives and a threat for business owners and stockholders. Company productivity and the national economy will markedly decline over time if executives allow this trend to continue. Fortunately, there are specific management approaches that can help motivate employees to produce at their best.

In the March 2004 issue of *Fortune* magazine, Wal-Mart was ranked number one on the Fortune 500 list for 2003, for the third straight year. Wal-Mart has not only become successful through offering quality products at discount prices, but also by the way it motivates its employees. When Wal-Mart's founder Sam Walton passed away in 1992, many people doubted that Wal-Mart could go on as a prominent discount retailer. Little did they know that Wal-Mart would climb up to the number one spot with record growth, revenues, and earnings.

Many experts believe that one of the key factors contributing to Wal-Mart's success is how it motivates its employees. Although Mr. Walton might not be around anymore, his famous employee "prep rally" meetings still energize the sales force before every new day's deluge of customers arrive. Ongoing computerized feedback data empower the sales force to key in on what the customer wants and how much they buy. Wal-Mart employs a sophisticated information technology system that is so advanced that it can provide up-to-the-minute details on sales on all products throughout all its stores. Worldwide, Wal-Mart is second only to the U.S. government in the amount of their information storage capacity of 24 terabytes! With real time data, the sales personnel can instantly compare how they did the previous day, week, month, or year.

The sales figures are not announced in a dry dull tone but with great excitement and fun. It is the little things that count. One store in Texas awarded a package of Oreo cookies to the employee who guessed closest to the number of items sold in the last two days. This type of presentation takes something quite ordinary and makes it extraordinary. It creates a sense of camaraderie and fun, which often defines the working experience at Wal-Mart.

With both the real-time information on sales and prep rallies, the management knows that the employees are equipped with the resources necessary to do their very best. This is one of the keys to Wal-Mart's monumental success.[3]

You may be thinking, "Well, that's Wal-Mart, come on!" But the underlying principles are the same for all businesses. Even a small mom-and-pop store can creatively implement the key principles that Wal-Mart uses to motivate employees.

Many appealing recommendations have been proposed on how managers can motivate employees, but not all these ideas are actually effective. What, then, makes some methods effective and others not? Scientific research in the field of Organizational Behavior (OB) can now be applied to management practices in order to effectively motivate employees. Managers should ask, "What motivates people and why?" Then once they discover the answer, they should ask, "How can I put it to use?"

Let's start with a definition. *Motivation* is "a set of processes that arouse someone to maintain some human behavior directed to accomplishing some goal."[4]

Two key points about motivation stand out from OB research:

1. motivation is not synonymous with job performance, and
2. money is not the only factor that motivates people.

Understanding motivation is vitally important to your organization for the essential purposes of retaining employees and maximizing their productivity. Some managers follow a common rule: Assume what motivates *you* motivates others.[5]

Frederick Taylor, the father of Scientific Management, claimed, "What workers want most from their employers, beyond anything else, is high wages." But research has shown that employees seek meaning and satisfaction from their jobs in addition to money. So the most effective managers find out exactly what motivates their employees and then supply those incentives.

Astute managers show great interest in some recent research done on the topic of what motivates employees that was conducted by Dr. Chip Heath, an associate professor at Stanford University. Heath found that managers are not particularly good at determining what motivates employees. In fact, many misunderstand what really drives employees to perform at their best.

Heath's research discovered the "extrinsic incentives bias." Extrinsic incentives bias refers to our tendency to think that people are motivated by external rewards such as pay, benefits, and job security rather than intrinsic rewards such as a feeling of belonging, desire to learn, and a feeling of contribution to the organization. Heath's research found that the assumption that employees are primarily motivated by extrinsic rewards is false.

In one of Heath's tests, he asked 25 managers at Citibank to pick 30 of their subordinates and rate the value they put on extrinsic and intrinsic rewards. Heath discovered that the managers significantly underestimated the value of intrinsic rewards and overestimated the value of extrinsic rewards. This study reveals why some managers have fallen short, or are way off the mark in motivating their staff. But this same information can have a big impact on how astute managers approach the challenge of motivating their employees in the future.

The University of Chicago's National Opinion Research Center conducted the General Social Survey (GSS), which examined work issues. This research obtained a random sample of the U.S. adult population and then asked them to rank in importance these five aspects of their job: free time, security, pay, chances for advancement, and the opportunity to do "important work that gives a feeling of accomplishment."

The majority of the people surveyed ranked "important work" the highest in importance for themselves. Surprisingly, pay was third. But paradoxically, when the applicants where then asked what motivates other people the most, one-third said that pay makes the largest difference in motivating people to work. This research indicates that pay is a less important motivator when workers report on *their own* motivation. But it also suggests that it is common to assume that pay is the most important motivator of other people.

When the manager's view of what motivates employees does not fit how the employees are truly motivated, then that manager develops incentives that do not meet employee needs. Although money does have a large effect on motivation, managers must understand that this is not the only factor that motivates employees, and, in fact may not even be the most important. A sense of belonging and contribution to the organization are motivating to employees and can have a huge effect on their level of productivity.

At the Gold Medal Level, there is an ideal atmosphere for "A" employees. All employees are excited to accomplish results and to be effective in the company.

This is where you want to be! Employees are excited to come to work and management becomes much easier due to the overwhelmingly positive atmosphere. At this top level, managers have a full understanding of what their employees' needs are, what they can do to meet those needs, and have implemented practices that meet their employees' needs. This maximizes employee motivation.

"All hard work brings a profit...."[6]

Dynamic Fifteen: Motivate Your Workforce		
Score	Level	Description
☐ 1-5	Endangered Survivor Level	Employees feel fear and pressure. Managers believe that employees are basically lazy and untrustworthy needing direct orders, close supervision, and regular reminders that noncompliance will have certain negative consequences.
☐ 6-10	Struggling Survivor Level	An employee discipline program is in place, but praise and other incentives are very rarely given, even for high productivity.
☐ 11-15	Enduring Survivor Level	Employees are evaluated at least annually and managers attempt to meet some of the needs of the employees. But praise and monetary rewards are given only after the most exceptionally outstanding performance of an employee.

DYNAMIC FIFTEEN: MOTIVATE YOUR WORKFORCE		
SCORE	LEVEL	DESCRIPTION
☐ 16-20	BRONZE MEDAL LEVEL	Employee development is included in annual performance evaluations. Executive managers encourage good performance with praise and effective incentives.
☐ 21-25	SILVER MEDAL LEVEL	All employees and top leaders are regularly evaluated and provided development opportunities. Employees are promoted based on objective evaluation criteria. A positive culture of praise and promotion is in practice throughout the company, in addition to effective compensation packages.
☐ 26-30	GOLD MEDAL LEVEL	The company is the ideal atmosphere for "A" employees. All employees are highly motivated to accomplish measured results and to be effective in the company. Managers create a positive environment that encourages the intrinsic motivation of the employees to excel. Managers evaluate performance, but trust employees to be productive.

DYNAMIC SIXTEEN

INSPIRE A GOAL-ORIENTED WORKFORCE

"You measure the size of an accomplishment by the obstacles you have to overcome to reach your goals."

—BOOKER T. WASHINGTON[1]

To maximize your company's success you need employees who work together effectively. Your company should have its overarching goals guided by a clear vision of where it wants to be in the future. In order to realize those goals, you must inspire your workforce to develop and identify with their individual and group goals that are essential for realizing that vision.

Your employees need to know *generally* what you expect from them, and with that in mind, each employee needs to set his or her own *specific* measurable goals in collaboration with management. Having a goal-oriented workforce gives your employees a game plan, which, in turn motivates them and helps them be more productive. Challenging employees to set and focus on goals helps them think more creatively. This collaboration between employees and their managers results in more effective goal-setting than what the managers could accomplish alone.

Companies with a goal-oriented workforce tend to have fewer hierarchical levels and the employees are more empowered to solve problems. These companies are typically decentralized; success is not commanded from the top but rather from the bottom. The employees are the ones serving on the front lines who have the best access and detailed know-how to solve problems much more effectively than a distant manager.

Employees who contribute in goal setting take greater ownership in the goals and are more willing to work hard to accomplish the goals because they helped establish them. Thus, your employees become something like a network of "one-person-entrepreneurs" all working together throughout the business.

By the time your company reaches the Silver Medal Level, every employee is involved in setting their own goals and strategies that will help the whole company realize its overarching goals. In this way, the company affirms the human dignity of their employees and has included their thinking as well as their specific work. This enables each employee:

- ❖ to experience a level of self-determination,
- ❖ to enjoy the opportunity to unfold their own potential,
- ❖ to discuss and negotiate larger goals rather than mere disconnected work details, and
- ❖ to be empowered as a valued problem-solver.

Then at the Gold Medal Level, all employee salaries and bonuses directly depend on their achievement of their individual goals. Every employee is a co-bearer in the business risks. Every employee has incentives (increase/decrease of wages, salary, or bonuses) for achieving their goals. In a sense, this allows the employees to function something like co-owners in the business because when they achieve their goals that contribute to business success, they not only receive intrinsic rewards, but monetary reward as well. But if they don't achieve goals, they do not prosper as much.

An ancient book of wisdom says, "Plans fail for lack of counsel, but with many advisors they succeed."[2] In a company with a goal-oriented workforce, employees become "advisors" to your business. With this increased level of input, you make wiser decisions.

> *"All success is based on agreement...if colleagues don't agree or believe our work has value, we won't get very far. Realize that people will grant our request when those requests appeal to their self-interest. They will give you what you want. But you must give first."*
>
> —THOMAS J. NEVINS[3]

Dynamic Sixteen: Inspire a Goal-oriented Workforce		
Score	**Level**	**Description**
☐ 1-5	Endangered Survivor Level	Senior management gives commands, sets all the goals, and expects the workforce to get authorization from their immediate supervisor for any change from the specific orders of management.
☐ 6-10	Struggling Survivor Level	Your workforce is able to identify how their strengths are being used to fulfill the overall company motto or emphasis. But senior management still sets all the company goals.
☐ 11-15	Enduring Survivor Level	Your company has an annual leadership group meet to set goals and the strategies for reaching them.

Dynamic Sixteen: Inspire a Goal-oriented Workforce		
Score	**Level**	**Description**
☐ 16-20	Bronze Medal Level	In addition to an annual leadership strategy retreat, the chief executive has at least quarterly meetings with each member of the leadership team individually, to set and fine-tune goals and strategies to reach them.
☐ 21-25	Silver Medal Level	Every employee is involved with their manager in setting their own goals. They participate in developing strategies that will contribute to reaching the overarching goals of the entire company.
☐ 26-30	Gold Medal Level	All employee salaries and bonuses directly depend on the achievement of their individual goals. Every employee is a co-bearer in the business risks and company productivity.

Dynamic Seventeen

Empower and Coach Employees

"To lead the people, walk behind them."

—Lao Tzu, 2,500 years ago[1]

Steve Rayner astutely observed, "Historically, corporations have limited employee involvement by narrowly defining jobs, filtering information, maintaining tight spans of control, and concentrating decision making, responsibility, and authority in the upper echelons of management."[2]

Reflecting this out-dated management mentality, in many of today's businesses, people are hired and paid only to work and not to think. These employees have many fine human qualities that can be seen in their lives outside of work. But too often, during work hours, those qualities are not valued.

Outstanding executives realize that all their employees have valuable capacities to solve company problems. When your employees are empowered and their intellectual potential unleashed, companies often experience tremendous improvements in their performance.

Two dominant themes surface in Kenneth Blanchard and Spencer Johnson's book, *The One Minute Manager*. The first is that the quality of time spent with subordinates is more important than the quantity. The second theme is that people should ultimately be managing themselves.[3] Empowering your employees helps accomplish this second objective of employee self-management. Coaching them implements both themes.

The best type of employees prefer to contribute their ideas and creativity instead of merely functioning like a little wheel in the clockwork. If you empower employees with access to all company information related to their job, they will be gratified to contribute their thoughts about performance improvements and optimization. The successful steel maker Nucor pushes authority down their organizational structure to managers and frontline employees, so that they will have the opportunity to fully use their talents and abilities. Thus, employees know that they are empowered and expected to be trying out new ideas and practices, and increasing performance, cutting costs, influencing members of the team to produce greater effort.[4] The decentralization and empowerment policies of successful companies like Valspar (a paint and coverings company) and Nucor (a steel company) are partly intended to encourage good employees to stick around.[5]

According to a report of the American Society for Training and Development, U.S. companies invest more than $44 billion in training their employees.[6] Such training contributes to empowering employees to make even greater contributions to their company's mission. Training includes formal classroom instruction, simulated work performance, formal apprenticeship programs, cross-cultural training, executive training programs, corporate "universities," and other formal and informal teaching situations. Training can become more effective if the approach is matched appropriately to what needs to be learned and matched to the individuals being trained.

Training your employees on the job is one of W. Edward Deming's fourteen points for transforming an organization.[8] Professors Greenberg and Baron appropriately proposed that training can be more effective when [1] the learners can participate in the learning process, [2] opportunity for repeated practice is offered and spread over time, [3] transfer of training is sought through simulation of the actual job conditions and equipment, and [4] feedback information is provided to the learner so he or she can obtain specific knowledge of the results of specific actions.

One feedback approach is the 360-degree method to increasing management performance. This method is called "360-degree feedback" because a management consultant or executive coach gets feedback from individuals that surround the manager on all sides. The consultant or coach not only obtains feedback from the people reporting to the manager, but also the people to whom the manager reports.[7]

Once your company reaches the Gold Medal Level, a traditional improvement proposal system is no longer needed because your employees are empowered to work independently on their proposed improvement solutions. Employees recognize problems and come up with the solutions on their own. Each employee is authorized to spend company financial resources within a previously determined limit. Thus, each employee is empowered by management to be a problem solver.

Dan Bollom, CEO of Wisconsin Public Service, astutely observed, "Leaders are becoming more like coaches than directors."[9] The continual development of employees through coaching from their managers has become very efficient and effective. And many top executives receive outside coaching to maximize their capacity for top performance.

"Listen to advice and accept instruction, and in the end you will be wise."[10] At the Gold Medal Level, you are continuously putting this wisdom into practice.

"Never tell people how to do things. Tell them what to do and they will surprise you with their ingenuity."

—George S. Patton

Dynamic Seventeen: Empower and Coach Employees		
Score	Level	Description
☐ 1-5	Endangered Survivor Level	Your company has no organized system for employees to propose improvements. Management does not routinely invite employees to use their problem solving abilities to enhance company processes.
☐ 6-10	Struggling Survivor Level	Although your company has no formal improvement proposal system, some of your employees in the more responsible positions propose improvements in company procedures.
☐ 11-15	Enduring Survivor Level	Your company has an improvement proposal system. Some employees occasionally use it to make some proposals.

Dynamic Seventeen: Empower and Coach Employees		
Score	**Level**	**Description**
☐ 16-20	Bronze Medal Level	A structured improvement proposal system is well established and used by a variety of employees of your company. A few Continual Improvement Process teams are in place. All top executives receive outside coaching to maximize their capacity for top performance.
☐ 21-25	Silver Medal Level	The improvement proposal system of your company is well promoted and used regularly by employees. More than half of the employees regularly participate in Continual Improvement Process teams. In addition to outside coaching received by executives, the company managers regularly coach their employees.
☐ 26-30	Gold Medal Level	In your company, the traditional improvement proposal system is no longer needed because your employees work independently on their proposed improvement solutions. All executives, managers, and all other employees receive either outside or internal coaching to maximize personal effectiveness and corporate productivity.

Dynamic Eighteen

Build Effective Teams

"Teams are the Ferraris of work design. They're high performance but high maintenance and expensive."

—Author Unknown[1]

Increasingly, companies are using groups and teams. Why is this the case? What are the benefits of teams? And what are the potential problems you might encounter with groups and how can they be overcome? How are effective groups formed?[2]

A *group* is "a collection of two or more individuals who interact with a stable relationship, who share a common goal, and distinguish themselves as being in a group."[3] *Group dynamics* deal with the overall nature of groups such as how they are formed, developed, maintained, structured, or relate with other groups or the organization itself.

Teamwork, on the other hand, refers to the use of teams or other special kinds of groups in which the members are committed to a precise goal and also share in the leadership of reaching that specific goal. Because there has been a growing trend to use groups and teams in companies, it is reasonable to consider whether specific types of groups or teams might enhance your organization's performance.[4]

Using a group for decision-making holds the potential of several advantages that can produce higher-quality decisions:

- ❖Compared to a single individual, several people potentially have greater knowledge of relevant data and have a larger number of potential insights. This can be useful in identifying and diagnosing a problem and in discovering its causes.
- ❖A group also potentially brings a larger number of alternative approaches and perspectives to consider in solving the diagnosed problem.
- ❖Group members can stimulate one another's ideas. The "whole is greater than the sum of its parts"—that is, interaction in a group can produce a creative idea that no single individual could have produced alone.
- ❖Once a solution is chosen, a group decision (compared to an individual decision) has the built-in advantage of more immediate understanding of the decision by those involved because they have processed the solution together.
- ❖In the process of putting the decision into practice, a group decision also has the potential advantage of greater commitment to the decision itself (compared to an individually-made decision), leading to a greater likelihood that it will be successfully implemented.

However, using a group for making a decision can pose several potential dangers or disadvantages:

- ❖One individual may dominate the group discussion process, thereby stifling other perspectives.

- ❖Group members who dislike meetings may cut the discussion short of fully exploring new and better alternatives.
- ❖Social pressures to conform or to avoid a disagreement may stifle creativity and produce "group think."
- ❖Rather than jointly pursuing a discussion to arrive at the best possible solution to a business problem, a group may suffer goal displacement. For example, a heated disagreement may arise and displace the original group goal with a sidetrack such as trying to win an argument for argument's sake or trying to "save face."

Once it reaches the Gold Medal Level, a company has a systematic approach for forming teams, and teams are deployed throughout the organization. At this top level, the organization effectively uses teams, from the formation of teams through to the adjouring of the team. The management supports teams by providing adequate material and human resources to carry out the mission and purpose of each team.

A manager's track record of reliability and trustworthiness leads to high levels of trust. A manager's considerable emotional investment in relationships with employees, greater frequency of interaction, and extending help builds trust.[5] It would be very worthwhile to assure that these factors are present as you form teams because trust apparently directly influences helping and cooperation and indirectly increases work performance.[6]

In 1995 at one of Nucor's mills, a visitor observed a manufacturing team assemble spangles of different shapes and sizes on strips of galvanized steel. He watched as they discovered a new way of tailoring the spangles by using air pressure to dry the steel after it had gone through its zinc bath. This discovery eliminated a whole separate process and substantially sped up the production process. When the team's discovery was conveyed to the plant manager Larry Roos, he laughed and then explained, "I find that happening all the time around here. There are many improvements in cost, quality, and production that are going on that I don't even know about. They just happen, and they don't have to be rubber-stamped."[7]

At one point from 1986 to 1996, Nucor was producing 980 tons of steel per employee per year while the industry average was only 420 tons. Also, Nucor's cost per ton of steel produced was only $60, while the industry average was $135. The CEO of Nucor, Ken Iverson, said this about empowering teams, "We give the worker the training and furnish the equipment, and then, in a real sense, the team is in business for itself."[8] Because Nucor has mobilized its employees and teams by empowering them and supporting them, the company has reaped huge dividends. The same can be true for your company.

> *"We aim to have long-term relationships with our customers, employees, and others interested in the company. Creating a friendly atmosphere encourages employees to work with management towards a shared goal and not in opposition. This benefits the customer, and a friendly atmosphere and team spirit are highly beneficial to productivity."*
> —a managing director quoted in a business case study by Laurence Holt[9]

Dynamic Eighteen: Build Effective Teams		
Score	**Level**	**Description**
☐ 1-5	Endangered Survivor Level	The company rarely, if ever, forms organized groups or teams to accomplish goals and/or to solve business problems.
☐ 6-10	Struggling Survivor Level	Your employees spontaneously work together on some tasks, but no ongoing formal teamwork is in place yet.
☐ 11-15	Enduring Survivor Level	Your company occasionally forms teams to develop business solutions.

Dynamic Eighteen: Build Effective Teams		
Score	Level	Description
☐ 16-20	Bronze Medal Level	Teams are understood to bring added value to the company and are regularly used primarily in only one area of the company.
☐ 21-25	Silver Medal Level	Effective teams are created and regularly deployed to accomplish goals and solve business problems in more than one area of the company.
☐ 26-30	Gold Medal Level	The company has a systematic approach for forming teams. Teams effectively function throughout the entire organization.

GOAL FOUR:

CREATE LOYAL EMPLOYEES

Dynamic Nineteen

Value Your Workforce

"The biggest tragedy in America is not the great waste of natural resources, though this is tragic. The greatest tragedy is the waste of human resources. The average person goes to his grave with his music still in him."

—Oliver Wendell Homes[1]

Someone once said, "The success of a business is equal to the sum of the successes of its employees." If your employees are not successful, then how can your business succeed?

Not only is it important to hire the best employees, but it is also essential to treat them with the level of respect that makes them want to stay to advance your company. Keeping highly motivated and productive employees is a key ingredient of a recipe for business success.

Thus, executives must highly value their workforce and take specific actions to inspire them to be successful in order for a business to have any chance at succeeding in the long run. In his national best-seller, *Good to Great,* Jim Collins writes, "People are not your most important asset. The right people are."[2]

Your employees have needs that can be met, resulting in a "win-win" situation for them and for management. Good employees are always looking for more ways to be more efficient at their job and appreciate praise and recognition for their contribution to the organization. They like to be able to see how their efforts help the company succeed.

When you genuinely value your employees and fulfill their needs, they are more inclined to contribute to the success of your business. The more openly you express your appreciation for their contributions to your company, the better their performance will be.

Recall that, increasingly, many employees will not work for monetary compensation alone. Employees today put more and more emphasis on intrinsic rewards in addition to tangible extrinsic rewards.

In a company at Gold Medal Level, the employees find great significance in their work for the firm. They are treated with great trust and respect, which motivates them to take initiative and share work responsibilities with one another.

Joyce Goodman, employment director for 20th Century Fox had this to say about this critical matter:

> "Without trust and genuine interest by the executive, creativity and growth are stifled, and if subordinates only give executives back what they seem to want, they waste people and talent."[3]

Top executives highly value their employees. Managers are constantly seeking for new and creative ways of meeting and exceeding their employees' needs and wants. People join and want to stay with the company because of the meaningful work, team environment, and the positive work environment that is permeated by encouragement and praise. Such a company's culture is perfect for attracting "A" employees.

For the majority of employees, the weekend is the time for self-fulfillment. But in a Gold Medal Level company, the employee also finds fulfillment and appreciation in the workplace by being enabled to take on responsibilities that bring joy in his or her work.

In such an environment, employees take full responsibility for their own mistakes and the company culture is based on this kind of honesty and integrity. This provides trust and meaning to the work that is done.

When there is meaning in the employees' work, they have a greater internal drive to perform. The employees take more initiative and personally identify as a vital part of the company.

One of the most difficult tasks for managers is letting well-trained employees go—laying them off during downsizing. Some say that there is no way to guarantee that no one will be laid off. Or has some benchmark-level company found a way?

Founded by three engineers, Craig Nelson, Scott Young, and Neal Vaoifi, Mission Controls Automation was formed in 1997. The founders made a promise from day one that if worst came to worst, they would go without pay before they would lay off any of their employees. The founders knew first hand how devastating lay offs can be because they themselves had been "downsized" several times.

Nelson frankly stated, "People are always talking at the executive level about how hard it is to lay off staff, but from the employee's standpoint, it changes so much in your life. Losing a job affects everything from what college you can send your kids to, to what vacations you are able to take. It causes trauma to marriages and to families."

In Mission Controls' project-based industry, the standard practice is to hire and fire as contracts come and go. But the founders of Mission Controls decided to do things very differently. Nelson believes that other companies lay off because "most of the time they're just trying to protect salaries for top management." Mission Controls has made it clear to their 35 employees that the founders will go without salaries before cutting their jobs.

One time when things got tough, the three founders went without salary for eight months. Nelson proclaims proudly, "During that time, there were no reductions in benefits or other people's salaries." Nelson explains that today, "It seems like companies will do whatever they need to in order to turn a profit, but at the expense of people."

Mission Controls Automation highly values their workforce. In return, their employees are highly loyal and put in extra effort to make the company more profitable because they know that the company is taking care of them. They have significant job security in an otherwise shaky industry. "Very little of our success comes from the owners' being smart," Nelson says. "The biggest part is trusting employees to get us to do the smart thing." The company's hire-for-life culture creates loyal employees who stay with the company through thick and thin.[4]

> *"Our employees are our most valuable asset. We depend upon their skill, creativity, and commitment."*
> —Richard Beatty & Nicholas Burkholder[5]

Dynamic Nineteen: Value Your Workforce		
Score	Level	Description
☐ 1-5	Endangered Survivor Level	Company managers view employees primarily as another necessary cost and are convinced that employees are not actually as productive as they could be.
☐ 6-10	Struggling Survivor Level	Company managers have begun to realize that they devote more time and attention to the material assets of the company than to the employees of the company.
☐ 11-15	Enduring Survivor Level	The managers of the company have interviewed their employees to discover their workplace needs. Their findings have guided them to implement solutions to meet some of those needs.

Dynamic Nineteen: Value Your Workforce		
Score	Level	Description
☐ 16-20	Bronze Medal Level	A central focus of your company is to meet as many needs and aspirations of your employees as possible.
☐ 21-25	Silver Medal Level	Your company effectively communicates and implements its foundational values such that employees with these same values join the company because they perceive a company environment that will enable them to flourish.
☐ 26-30	Gold Medal Level	Your employees find great significance in their work at your company. They are treated with trust and great respect, which motivates them to take initiative and gladly assist one another.

Dynamic Twenty

Manage Stress

"Stress is normal and results from any situation that places a demand on you to readjust. But stress may become physically or emotionally harmful if its level is too high to handle or if the stress becomes continual. That's when stress actually becomes 'distress.'"

—Dr. George A. Rekers, professor and psychologist, University of South Carolina

The experience of stress does not depend upon whether a situation is positive or negative. Instead, what causes stress is the degree to which the situation places a demand on you to readjust or adapt. The manager who receives a big promotion must readjust to a pleasant change, while the person who loses a huge business deal has to readjust to a disappointing loss. Both of these individuals will experience stress because both must readjust to something significant to them. Whether the stressor is pleasant or unpleasant, your body's reaction to stress is essentially the same.

Henry Ford, one of the most famous innovators and industrialists of all times, founded the Ford Motor Company. His goal was simply stated, but highly innovative, "I will build a motor car for the multitude...so low in price that the man of moderate means may own one and enjoy with his family the blessings of happy hours spent in God's great open spaces."[1]

Ford definitely experienced some significant stress as an entrepreneur. He contended with an almost fatal legal battle initiated by George Selden and his group, who held a previously awarded patent for "road locomotives." Although it caused him considerable stress, Ford fought really hard in court and won the right to build his automobiles without having to pay any royalty payments to the Selden group. Ford transformed our world through his innovative use of an assembly line, thereby "sparking" production line efficiencies to produce low-cost products.

Ford also recognized the need for his workers to be relieved from their heavy work stresses every week. So he introduced a 5-day labor policy, explaining, "Every man needs more than one day for rest and recreation."[2]

Have you ever noticed that some people thrive on stress? Most young people love to ride roller coasters, skateboard down steep ramps, or play vigorous athletic games. Many firefighters would prefer to be out fighting fires and saving lives instead of passively waiting in the fire station. Many trial lawyers prefer the heat of conflict in the courtroom to calmly preparing for a trial in their office. Typically, a checkout clerk at a cash register would rather have a steady stream of customers to process rather than to idly sit there hour after hour with only a very few customers to help. Why is this the case? It is because the stress created is invigorating or entertaining.

Unfortunately, however, *distress* has mushroomed in the workplace, documented by numerous surveys. "A Northwestern National Life Insurance survey found in 1991 that 46 percent of U.S. workers described their jobs as highly stressful, twice as many as in 1985. Thirty-four percent of U.S. workers said they considered quitting their jobs in 1990 because of excessive stress; and 14 percent did quit their jobs because of excessive stress."[3] This excessive stress is really "distress." Executives need to recognize the difference between stress and distress in their employees and then take action to relieve and prevent distress.

Even when you sleep at night, your dreams cause you a certain amount of stress. It is an accepted scientific fact that the only way you can become completely free of all stress is to die. So don't make the mistake of asking someone to relieve you of all your stress! Stress is inevitably part of just being alive.

So you can not relieve all of your stress. But managers can teach employees four steps to reduce their stress and worry:

- ❖ *Stop.* When you encounter stress, you need to stop and pause before your worrying starts to imagine the worst, most catastrophic scenario that could happen. Just saying, "Stop!" to yourself can interrupt a pattern of worry and keep the negative stress cycle from being activated.
- ❖ *Breathe.* After stopping, take a deep breath and exhale it to release bodily tension. You might not realize it, but most people who encounter heightened stress initially tend to hold their breath. But some slow deep breathing can calm and relax you instead of activating a bodily stress response.
- ❖ *Reflect.* Now that you have stopped your usual automatic worrying and negative stress cycle, you can focus your energy on creatively solving the problem at hand. And you can reflect on what seems to be the threat to you that kicked in the stress response. This is the time to check if your thoughts are realistic. Ask yourself: Am I seeing this change as a catastrophe instead of a challenge? Am I starting to feel alienated instead of staying committed to being involved? Am I starting to feel hopeless and helpless instead of having a sense of control? Should I be turning to someone to

help me? Would it be more constructive to pray about the matter that seems out of my control instead of worrying about it?

- *Choose.* After you have stopped yourself from reacting in some negative automatic way to the stress, it is time to choose a strategy for coping with the stress. You can choose to not dwell on factors outside your control. Instead, choose constructive ways to think about and to deal with the difficult circumstance so you can rebound from that circumstance.

A company at the Gold Medal Level offers on-going stress management programs and stress hardiness coaching to all employees.

Consider the life of the famous business executive, Andrew Carnegie. Was Carnegie a stress-hardy businessman or someone excessively vulnerable to stress?

On November 25, 1835, Andrew Carnegie was born in Dunfermline, Scotland to a family of "Damask" linen weavers. According to one account, the Carnegies were so poor that they couldn't even feed their rabbits a decent meal. So Andrew would round up his friends and they would go out to gather vegetation to feed the rabbits. In return, he named a newborn bunny after each friend that helped gather food. At a very young age, Andrew learned that people are willing to work hard if they feel personally involved with the outcome.

In 1848, the Carnegies went through some hard times due to the invention of factory-automated looms. So the Carnegie family set out for America. Upon arriving in Pittsburgh with only pennies in their pockets, they started working in a loom factory. Andrew, age 13, worked hard in the loom factory as a "bobbin boy." Then he landed a job as a telegraph operator. He was the third person in the country to be able to decode a telegraph by listening rather than translating the message from the printed dots and dashes.

Andrew was a strong believer in art, religion, and politics. At the age of 20, he published an article in New York's *Weekly Tribune* against slavery. During the Civil War, Andrew rebuilt and repaired many telegraph stations and railroads. For a while, he even worked in the offices of U.S. President Abraham Lincoln.

But, after suffering extreme exhaustion, Carnegie learned that people need to rest their bodies and remember to enjoy life. Applying this insight as a manager, Carnegie was known for his kind intention to do the best for his employees. "Head service or hand service, it is heart service that counts," Carnegie was known to say.

During the depression in 1873, Carnegie went through some very difficult times with the crash of the nation's financial system. Believing that the economy would bounce back sooner or later, Carnegie decided to work without pay. Sure enough, he was right and he emerged even wealthier than before.

He went on to become one of the wealthiest men in America. When he died, most of his $300,000,000 fortune, which was worth substantially more in the nineteenth century than the same sum today, was given away to various charities around the world. He is known as an entrepreneur who spawned the growth of a nation.[4]

Dr. Suzanne Kobasa, a psychologist at the University of Chicago, and her colleague, Dr. S. R. Maddi, conducted a number of important studies that compared people who are stress resistant to those who develop emotional and health problems under stress.[5] Other researchers found that stress resistance increases with social support (closeness to supportive family and friends), devout Christian living, and taking good care of one's body (regular exercise, not smoking, and not overusing alcohol). In addition to these findings, Dr. Kobasa discovered the three characteristics of "stress-hardiness"—*challenge*, *commitment*, and *control*.

Andrew Carnegie's life illustrates these three characteristics of stress-hardy individuals who cope well under stress.

From a young age, Carnegie became *committed to involvement*, by getting friends to help him gather food for his rabbits. He was open to change, and viewed his condition of poverty as a *challenge* to work hard and advance himself in factory and telegraph work.

Carnegie's life also showed openness to change in the way he responded to the Civil War and the depression of 1873. He was flexible in moving from telegraph operating, to telegraph and railroad repair, and work for the U.S. President. When necessary, he was even willing to work without pay, making the decision himself, which indicates he had a sense of *control* even at times of heightened stress.

Unlike many business executives of today, Andrew Carnegie had the three qualities found in stress-hardy individuals. On the other hand, one indicator that he briefly struggled with some damaging effects of stress was his episode of suffering extreme exhaustion. But from this experience Carnegie learned an important lesson: Rest, exercise, and recreation are important for handling the stresses encountered in business.

> *"We can not control whether or not we have stress, but we can control how we react to stress."*
>
> —Matthew G. Rekers, CEO of 33Dynamics LLC

Dynamic Twenty: Manage Stress		
Score	**Level**	**Description**
☐ 1-5	Endangered Survivor Level	The effects of psychological stress are virtually ignored, overlooked, or simply not addressed by managers and employees in the company. Stress becomes "distress" for enough employees to significantly reduce the overall productivity of the company.
☐ 6-10	Struggling Survivor Level	Management is beginning to become aware of the production slowdown effects of stress on themselves and their employees. However, very little or no management action is taken to lower stress in the workplace.
☐ 11-15	Enduring Survivor Level	Stress management training is provided only to company managers or selected employees. There is a growing realization that a stress management program for more employees would also be beneficial.

Dynamic Twenty: Manage Stress		
Score	**Level**	**Description**
☐ 16-20	Bronze Medal Level	In addition to stress management training for all company managers, the managers have introduced some features of stress awareness and stress management for all employees. There is a clear realization by all employees that they will always have some level of stress but that it is "distress" that must be eliminated. A few opportunities per year are provided for the workforce to participate in recreation and relaxation together.
☐ 21-25	Silver Medal Level	The stress management program of your company is a permanent policy put in writing. It is offered to all employees, and supports every individual involved at the company. A variety of opportunities are provided throughout the year for the workforce to relax together, creating a positive, caring work environment.
☐ 26-30	Gold Medal Level	On-going stress management programs and stress hardiness coaching are provided to all employees. A variety of opportunities for workers to relax or exercise are provided on an ongoing regular basis.

Dynamic Twenty-One

Offer Job Enrichment

"We are discovering that we have two types of people: those who know more and more about less and less—the 'specialists'—and those who know less and less about more and more—the 'generalists.' If this continues, we'll soon have a world in which one group knows everything about nothing, while the other group understands nothing about everything."

—Eric Sevareid[1]

Business professors Greenberg and Baron cited a study that discovered that individuals who experienced *job rotation* relatively early in their careers were the best-performing employees. Compared to employees who had not experienced job rotation, those who *were* rotated ended up receiving the highest salaries and achieving the most rapid promotions. Job rotation enables employees to master a wider variety of skills, thereby enriching their work through variety.

The drawbacks of providing opportunities for job rotation are usually minimal. But in some cases, an employee might be rotated to a job that does not match his or her personality or capabilities. Thus, they might not be able to master the requisite skills. This could frustrate the worker and give that person a poor reputation in the eyes of their supervisor.[2]

On the positive side, by rotating jobs, employees learn additional procedures and competencies. They enhance their qualifications and increase their value to the business. The resulting cross-trained workforce enables managers to respond with flexibility to worker shortages caused by sickness, vacations, and other leaves of absence. This prevents costly delays in delivery dates. It also reduces the need to employ additional temporary or permanent personnel.

The skills acquired through job rotation empower the employee to function in a valuable new capacity. Now the employee becomes one who is—in increasing measure—responsible for the company's success.

When the most successful executives add to their employees' learning by offering job rotation, they serve as a source of guidance for their employees. The executive leadership is no longer perceived as the "ruling caste." Instead, executives become encouragers and supporters of their employees. Such leaders help their employees to develop their potential and to increase their productivity by taking on a wider range of responsibilities.

This new relationship between executives and employees, made possible through job rotation, is a recent research discovery of an ancient principle expressed in this proverb: "...let the wise listen and *add to their learning*, and let the discerning get guidance...."[3]

Upon reaching the Gold Medal Level, a company maintains a fully developed job enrichment program that includes job rotation and a work environment that is challenging, rewarding, and exciting. When vacancies occur in the workforce, the company has enough multi-tasked performers to immediately cover all critical job functions of the vacant positions.

At the Gold Medal Level, most, if not all, employees have the skills and cross-training to work in several areas of the company. Worker shortages caused by increased customer demand, illness, unanticipated resignations or retirements do not create a short-term problem.

A company with no employee turnover! Can you believe it? Since its founding in 1997, BitFlip Interactive Group located in New York City has had absolutely no employee turnover. And for a company that is in the Internet business, this is amazing to contemplate. How do they do it?

Erin Jurew who founded BitFlip Interactive Group says the secret is "respect for your employees. Realize you're not going to be in business without your employees—and show them loyalty." Jurew provides her employees with work that is highly creative and allows them to pick the projects and clients they wish to work with. "That keeps people interested," says Jurew. And keeping employees interested is a formula for keeping them around, Jurew discovered.

From the earliest stage of the hiring process, Jurew tries to ensure the best match between the job and the employee. "Ours is a collaborative environment," says Jurew. She wants the new employees to fit into the company culture in two ways: (1) in skill and (2) in personality. Another reason why her 15 employees stick around so long is because they are offered perks such as excellent retirement plans and profit sharing, which are not common in small businesses. BitFlip even has a ping-pong table for use during breaks, and the company has a movie night. Jurew believes that if you are loyal to your employees and enrich their job, they will become loyal to your company.[4] Jurew has led BitFlip to the Gold Medal Level of job enrichment by creating an overall work environment that is very challenging, intrinsically rewarding, exciting, and amply compensated with uncommon fringe benefits.

Eventually, even the highest functioning companies—including BitFlip Interactive Group—will experience some employee turnover. But job enrichment will minimize employee turnover. And when illnesses, retirements, or resignations inevitably occur, the cross-training and job rotation programs will ensure that the remaining employees will be fully equipped to immediately step in and perform the essential job functions of the missing employee. Thus your company will not "miss a beat." Instead, it can maintain its competitive advantage in the ever changing and ever demanding business world.

> *"Few things can help an individual more than to place responsibility on him, and to let him know that you trust him."*
>
> —Booker T. Washington, *Up from Slavery*

Dynamic Twenty-One: Offer Job Enrichment		
Score	**Level**	**Description**
☐ 1-5	Endangered Survivor Level	Your employees only work in one separate function. Management has not developed a set of policies or procedures for job rotation to be able to respond immediately to any job vacancies.
☐ 6-10	Struggling Survivor Level	Because of employee sicknesses, sudden job vacancies, and other labor shortages, company management has identified a few specific areas where job rotation could enhance company preparedness to maintain its level of productivity. But job rotation has not yet been implemented.
☐ 11-15	Enduring Survivor Level	Management organizes employees within a few specific departments to expand their qualifications through cross-training for job rotation.

Dynamic Twenty-One: Offer Job Enrichment		
Score	**Level**	**Description**
☐ 16-20	Bronze Medal Level	Every department of your company has an extensive job cross-training program that equips its employees to perform new job functions. You have identified and recorded the multiple qualifications of each employee for alternate job assignments when needed.
☐ 21-25	Silver Medal Level	You have employees who cross-train one another to perform multiple job functions not only within their own department but also across other departments of your company.
☐ 26-30	Gold Medal Level	Your company has a fully implemented job enrichment program that includes widespread job rotation and a work environment that is challenging, rewarding, and exciting. When vacancies occur in your workforce, your company has enough multi-tasked performers to cover all critical job functions of all vacant positions.

Dynamic Twenty-Two

Promote Continuing Education

"Develop your people. Give to your people. Take care of your people. It remains the single greatest component of success and the most overlooked."

—David Collingham,
Indermaur International Limited[1]

"Learning is more important to your career than any raise or promotion."

—Ed Stephensen, Coca-Cola Company[2]

Microsoft founder, Bill Gates, told a TV interviewer that as CEO, if he fell asleep for half a year, he would wake up to find that Microsoft had fallen hopelessly behind the competition. Why?

Because today, to survive and thrive, all successful business must continually work hard to stay innovative and *dynamic*—that is, continually adapting to change with ever fresh competitive excellence. The globalization of markets and rapid technological change create a harsh reality: The company that stands still in a static stance will struggle to survive.

Peter Drucker predicted, "The typical organization will be knowledge-based, an organization composed largely of specialists who direct and discipline their own performance through organized feedback from colleagues, customers, and headquarters."[3] We live in an information age with rapid change, and in order to keep up, we must all continually learn. It has been estimated that the world's knowledge doubles every fifth year and its speed increases every year. Just to keep up with competition, companies need to keep educating their employees. There's no doubt about it: If a company wants to secure its competitive advantage, it must invest in education.

"Instruct a wise man and he will be wiser still; teach a righteous man and he will add to his learning."[4] This was very perceptive advice offered over two thousand years ago. And yet it is even more important in our time with the explosion of knowledge.

Because education has become so important for the success of business, corporate-sponsored training has become a large industry in the United States. Even employees realize quickly that to stay marketable in the ever-changing business world, they need to continually educate themselves to increase their level of qualifications. Such employees are willing to learn and to develop their skills when given the opportunity.

Continuing education produces improvements in operations. More knowledgeable employees are better equipped to work together to solve problems and accomplish tasks. More educated employees work better in teams and create synergy. In the team environment, there is a mutual exchange of knowledge and skills, which makes the organization a permanent learning center.

There is an oft-quoted story about Tom Watson, the founder of IBM. One of Tom's subordinates made a terrible mistake, which ended up costing the company $10 million. When that demoralized and embarrassed employee was called into Tom's office, he ashamedly avoided eye-to-eye contact, not lifting his gaze from the floor. He quietly muttered, "I suppose you want my resignation." Watson quickly replied, "Are you kidding? We just spent ten million dollars educating you!"[5]

Schering-Plough is a successful pharmaceutical company that produces and sells the popular allergy medicine, Claritin, as its best selling product. It provides an outstanding model of how a company can generously support the continuous education of its employees. This forward-looking company has training programs in areas ranging from management to sales, language classes, math, and secretarial skills. Schering-Plough offers to reimburse 90 percent of the tuition expense for all its managers and employees who decide to go back to college to take undergraduate or graduate level courses. For instance, the company has more than 2,000 employees who take courses in production practices every year.[6]

The popular business book, *What Really Works*, describes the groundbreaking Evergreen Project, a five-year study of the secrets of the world's best companies. This study identified Seagate Technology as a "winning company." Seagate is one of the world's largest manufacturers of disk drives. They provide full reimbursement for tuition costs to managers and employees who take college courses that are work-related. Because of this policy, about 40 percent of the company's workforce is enrolled in college courses. The company also offers their own courses in areas such as computer skills, English, and cross-cultural management. The authors of *What Really Works*—William Joyce, Nitin Nohria, and Bruce Roberson—discovered that Seagate's continuing education for employees produces beneficial results, "By investing in its international workforce, Seagate has been able to attract and retain the best talent across the globe."[7]

When a company reaches the Gold Medal Level, an environment exists in which effective practical teaching and learning are a continual aspect of corporate life. Every employee has the opportunity to participate with managers in decision-making about how to best further his or her education for self-development. As Seagate's experience indicates, the continuing education not only benefits the employee personally, but it also enhances company adaptability, productivity, and overall competitiveness.

The Gold Medal Level firm is a "learning company" where teaching and learning are an everyday part of the business. There is commitment to continual self-development through learning in every area of the company. This coincides with one of W. Edward Deming's fourteen points for transforming an organization: "Institute a vigorous program of education and self-improvement."[8]

At this level, the managers have guided the company to develop an environment where learning and education are the norm. Everyone in the company realizes their ongoing need for further education and improvement. They are eager to learn and continuously develop themselves to increase their value to the business. The employees play major roles in determining their own further education and in teaching other employees.

Not only is in-house business training offered to enhance the qualification level of employees, but the company also looks outside its walls and compares itself with the best practices in the industry in order to implement improvements for reaching and sustaining a leading market position.

> *"In every area of your life—keep learning. And never ever stop learning new things, always push yourself to learn."*
> —David Host, Allied Signal[9]

Dynamic Twenty-Two: Promote Continuing Education		
Score	Level	Description
☐ 1-5	Endangered Survivor Level	Executives think that because your employees and managers have worked satisfactorily for your company for some time, this work experience is qualification enough for them and for the company. It is assumed that the company does not need to provide employees with any further education or training to work for the enterprise.
☐ 6-10	Struggling Survivor Level	Your company has a limited amount of continuing education provided to the top managers, but none for middle and line managers nor for rank and file employees.
☐ 11-15	Enduring Survivor Level	The employee development and continuing education of your company is focused primarily on upper and middle management and selected department leaders. There is no systematic approach to developing all the other employees in the company.

Dynamic Twenty-Two: Promote Continuing Education		
Score	Level	Description
☐ 16-20	Bronze Medal Level	Continuing education in your company is strategically planned and offered to all managers. The strengths of each employee have been identified to effectively match training to employee aptitudes. These trained employees are beginning to be placed according to their strengths.
☐ 21-25	Silver Medal Level	Your company has its own ongoing educational process for all employees. All employees are placed according to a match of their individual strengths and training to the requirements of specific jobs.
☐ 26-30	Gold Medal Level	A company environment exists in which effective practical teaching and learning are a continual aspect of corporate life. Every employee has the opportunity to participate in decision-making about how to best further his or her education. These company practices promote self-development that further enhances employee satisfaction, company adaptability, productivity, and overall competitiveness.

DYNAMIC TWENTY-THREE

CREATE EMPLOYEE CO-OWNERSHIP

"The biggest disease today is not leprosy or tuberculosis, but rather the feeling of being unwanted, uncared for, and deserted by everybody. The greatest evil is the lack of love and charity—the terrible indifference towards one's neighbor who lives at the roadside assaulted by exploitation, corruption, poverty, and disease."

—MALCOLM MUGGERIDGE[1], when he was with Mother Teresa in Calcutta

Happy workers are productive workers. Do you agree or disagree with this statement?

Scientific research has tested this statement and found it to be usually true. But surprisingly, this research found only a *weak* connection between being happy with one's job and the level of one's productivity.[2]

The success of your business depends, in large part, on high quality work by your employees. When they are rewarded well for their performance, they have the motivation to help improve your company, to increase your company's market flexibility, and to increase your company's effectiveness and productivity. When your employees' actions contribute to your business success, they should be fairly rewarded for their efforts.

"One man gives freely, yet gains even more; another withholds unduly, but comes to poverty."[3] It is possible to share your company's wealth with your employees and thereby gain even more wealth for the company. Some executives have been miserly and stingy, not properly compensating employees, only to discover in the long run that the company falters because of unmotivated workers and a high turnover rate. Short-term material gain from short-changing the workers can eventually lead to poverty, as the proverb warns.

If you offer your employees the financial rewards of functioning like "co-owners" in the business, they will be more willing to put forth their best efforts because they will share in the fruits of the business success.

Consider these sayings, "Do not muzzle the ox while it is treading out the grain," and, "The worker deserves his wages."[4]

Many centuries ago, the truth of the saying, "The worker deserves his wages,"[5] was recognized and acted upon by wise employers. They realized, as executives should also realize today, that when employers unfairly enrich themselves by not giving the workers the full compensation they deserve for their labor, they will eventually suffer a penalty for this injustice. This is one of those universal truths that are embedded in reality and written about in ancient wisdom literature. But thankfully, there is a solution available, "A generous man will prosper; he who refreshes others will himself be refreshed."[6]

There are many ways to increase employee satisfaction and help employees feel like they are a vital part of the company. Profit sharing is one way, while allowing for flexible work hours is another. Providing flexible working times gives employees more freedom to pursue their private obligations, interests, and hobbies.

Why should the employer provide flexible work hours to allow the employee freedom to accomplish his or her own private obligations? Because it is very practical to follow the advice, "Do to others as you would have them do to you."[7]

If you would like to have the freedom to schedule your work hours around your own personal tasks (and who wouldn't appreciate this freedom?), then you should do what you can to provide the same opportunity for your employees. This freedom is usually a benefit of being a co-owner of a business, and this benefit can be shared with employees through some orderly policies and procedures.

At the Gold Medal Level, a company has both a profit-sharing program and a stock-options program. Employees are rewarded on a performance basis. Every employee receives a profit-sharing payment in relation to his or her contribution to the company.

There is a system of recording work hours only if employees demand one. Your employees' work hours are determined by market demand. Employees function as co-entrepreneurs and shareholders in your company. Their interest in the success of the business has tremendously increased. Employees are treated and act like co-owners in the company.

The steel giant, Nucor, has a "sharing-the-pain policy" in which the bonuses of top executives are tied to the annual performance of the company. If the company does well the executives are compensated accordingly, and if the company profits fall, the executives' compensation shrinks accordingly. When Nucor's CEO Ken Iverson was asked if this was fair, he replied, "Absolutely! The general managers and the corporate management make the decisions that determine whether or not Nucor is successful. If we make wise decisions, we receive bonuses. If we make poor decisions that affects the entire company, we share the pain."[8]

More than 75 percent of the CEO's pay at Nucor is based on company performance. Bonuses or rewards are based on meeting specific percentages and dollar amounts for sales, growth, profits, and cash. This approach of compensating personnel on their performance can be a powerful motivator and has been found to be a characteristic of many of the top performing companies.[9]

"A wise servant will...share the inheritance as one of the brothers."[10]

> *"You can't out give God. His resources are fully reliable, abundant, and freely offered on your behalf."*
>
> —Mary Kay Ash, CEO, Mary Kay Inc.

Dynamic Twenty-Three: Create Employee Co-ownership		
Score	**Level**	**Description**
☐ 1-5	Endangered Survivor Level	Every employee is simply compensated by his/her wages or salary. There is a defined beginning and end to the scheduled work day for all employees. This policy is strictly enforced with no flexible working times offered or allowed.
☐ 6-10	Struggling Survivor Level	Your company has some form of profit-sharing, but only for the leading employees or top management. The number of work hours for a full-time workweek is defined. Overtime is only paid when employees in certain positions exceed the set number of hours of your normal full-time workweek.
☐ 11-15	Enduring Survivor Level	In a highly profitable year, bonuses and/or profit-sharing checks are awarded to the employees. Your company has introduced work time accounts that allow flexible work hours, movable time, and options for getting credit for overtime.

Dynamic Twenty-Three: Create Employee Co-ownership		
Score	**Level**	**Description**
☐ 16-20	Bronze Medal Level	Your employees all directly participate in the financial success of your company and are rewarded with bonuses at the end of more profitable periods. Flexible work times are available for employees on a fixed salary.
☐ 21-25	Silver Medal Level	Your company has a profit-sharing program and/or a stock-options program for all regular employees. Your work groups, comprised of employees with fixed salaries, determine the daily schedule of work hours for each employee.
☐ 26-30	Gold Medal Level	Your company has both a profit-sharing program and a substantial stock-options program for all regular employees. A system of recording work hours exists only if employees demand one, and the work hours of your employees are determined by customer demand.

GOAL FIVE:

ACHIEVE MARKET DOMINANCE

Dynamic Twenty-Four

Build on Your Core Competencies

"Our goals as we progress in life should be to do very well whatever it is we're doing. If I'm picking up garbage, I want to be the best garbage collector in the world. If I'm designing an integrated circuit, I want to be the best at that. Learn as much as you can, but set your aspirations to being really good at what you do and not always, but most of the time, the progression will take care of itself."

—George Fisher, Motorola Chairman[1]

In order to be successful, your company must have core competencies. Precisely what do we mean by the term "core competence"?

Business professors Bateman and Snell gave this answer: "Simply stated, core competence is something a company does especially well relative to its competitors. Honda, for example, has a core competence in small engine design and manufacturing; Sony has a core competence in miniaturization; Federal Express has a core competence in logistics and customer service. Typically, a core competence refers to a set of skills or experience in some activity, rather than physical or financial assets."[2]

Strong core competencies:

- ❖ are well-organized special skills, technologies, processes, knowledge, expertise, abilities.
- ❖ are typically achieved by long-term development processes and experiences.
- ❖ create customer value and are considered by your customers to be unique and distinguishable, and they are not equally accessible to all competitors.
- ❖ are extremely difficult for other companies to imitate, if they can at all.
- ❖ can be transferred to many other markets.

Microsoft has the core competence of designing office software products that are user-friendly. PepsiCo has a core competence of mass production and distribution of bottled drinks. Polaroid has a core competence in manufacturing immediately self-developing film. Ernst & Young has the core competence of performing audit functions for Fortune 500 corporations. One of Wal-Marts' core competencies is their massive "real-time" information system.

There are many different types of core competencies that make companies unique. Identifying and developing your company's core competencies are management keys to sustaining your company's long-term competitive advantage.

Your company's core competencies can be applied to the development of new and creative products or services and markets. Take Polaroid for example: before there was video recording, they could have hypothetically tried to develop an instantly developing video camera film from their then existing core competence. Microsoft could use its core competence to develop user-friendly video games. PepsiCo could use its core competence of bottling and distribution to bottle and distribute medicines or hair care products. Ernst & Young could use its core competence to develop a CPA review course. There are many different ways to develop your core competencies. In today's environment of intense global competition, your business must focus its time and resources on developing core competencies and then creatively applying them to an ever-changing market, to remain competitive.

So your core competence is what sets your company apart from other companies. What is *your* company's core competence? Think about the underlying skill, ability, knowledge, experience, technology, or process that enables your company to provide its unique set of products or services. How can you use your company's core competence to develop strategic responsiveness in order to gain competitive advantage? These are the kinds of practical questions that astute executives need to ponder.

The overall value delivered to your customers and the uniqueness of your company's products or services are derived from your company's core competence. Your company's core competence enables you to develop new products or services to meet ever-changing market demands. Thus, your core competence is like your secret to success.

At the Gold Medal Level, a company develops *new* core competencies as well as expanding existing ones in order to enter new and future markets. A company at this high level of functioning recognizes the needs and wants of customers in new and future markets and develops the competencies necessary to meet those needs and wants.

Nokia is a good example of a company performing at Gold Medal Level. Nokia, which traditionally manufactured rubber boots, developed new core competencies, ventured out, and now produces mobile phones. Nokia has been able to open up new markets by using their innovative technologies.

Nike is one of the most well known companies in the world. Its famous "swoosh" logo can be seen all over the world. The company learned a painful lesson in the 1990's when its market share dramatically fell in the United States. Joyce, Nohria, and Roberson summarized the lesson learned by Nike: "Even the most successful strategy will fail unless it is continuously monitored and refreshed to meet changing market conditions."[3]

Some companies are finding that they can more easily expand core competencies and develop new ones by hiring a diverse workforce that reflects the population demographics of the nation. Employing a diverse workforce can give an edge in keeping a pulse on the emerging demands of future markets. The pursuit of diversity enables companies to expand their potential talent pool, capitalizing on the full range of aptitudes, skills, and sub-cultural expertise available in the labor market. Presently, minorities and immigrants comprise one-fourth of the U.S. labor market, nonwhites account for 35% of the labor growth rate, and women make up about 47% of the workforce.[4]

Sheila Heinze is the president of SM Consulting, an IT consulting firm that has grown 625% in the past five years compared with an industry growth rate of only 31%. What sets SM Consulting apart from most other IT consulting firms?

Heinze would tell you that it is the time invested in research. SM Consulting sales staff members are required to know as much as possible about a prospect before they even pick up the phone. They are to find out the problems and challenges that the customer's company is going through. These practices have become even more important as SM Consulting started targeting new customers in a different industry segment.

"We were able to gain instant credibility by having knowledge of what his pains might be and some potential solutions to those pains," Heinze explained after her sales team met with a potential customer. One contact alone brought a $250,000 project that Heinze described as a "great potential for add-on business."

SM Consulting keeps developing core competencies as they expand into new industry segments. Having knowledgeable sales personnel who do their homework allows SM Consulting to obtain a competitive advantage and considerable success in a changing industry environment.[5]

> *"We live in a world where change is the only constant."*
> —THOMAS F. KELLER, Dean of Duke University's
> Fuqua School of Business[6]

Dynamic Twenty-Four: Build on Your Core Competencies		
Score	**Level**	**Description**
☐ 1-5	Endangered Survivor Level	Your company does not have any real core competencies.
☐ 6-10	Struggling Survivor Level	Core competencies do exist in your company, but they are not identified as such, and rarely, if ever, are considered as a factor in management decision-making.
☐ 11-15	Enduring Survivor Level	Company managers strategize business activities on the basis of an awareness of the core competencies of the company.

Dynamic Twenty-Four: Build on Your Core Competencies		
Score	**Level**	**Description**
☐ 16-20	Bronze Medal Level	Your company expands on the basis of its core competencies in order to stay competitive in your current market.
☐ 21-25	Silver Medal Level	Your company continually builds on its core competencies, innovates new products or services, and enters new markets where it can transfer its core competencies.
☐ 26-30	Gold Medal Level	Your company develops new core competencies as well as expanding existing ones in order to enter new and future markets.

DYNAMIC TWENTY-FIVE

FOCUS ON YOUR TARGET MARKET

"Don't buy market share. Figure out how to earn it."

—PHILIP KOTLER[1]

Hallmark is an outstanding example of a company that has focused on its target market well. Known for its greeting cards, Hallmark continuously introduces new lines of cards specifically targeting different market segments. For example, their *Fresh Ink* line targets women 18-39 years old, while *Hallmark En Espanol* targets Hispanics. Hallmark also has a line aimed at African-American customers called *Mahogany*. They have been notably successful in their focus on different market segments. In the year 2000, Hallmark had a 55 percent share in the global greeting-card market of $7.8 billion.[2]

You can compare a successful business to an outstanding athlete. Scott Tinley recalls his first triathlon in 1977. "I was doing different things: college, teaching sailing, working as a firefighter/paramedic, and managing a sailing center. I left a full-time job for a part-time job that was supplemented by a sponsorship deal that allowed me the same income level." In order to be successful at the triathlon, Scott had to focus his time specifically on training for that event. This is similar to what a business must do in order to be successful in a target market. Success comes only if the focus is on a specific area.

If you try to supply every demand of every customer, you will quickly discover that your company is not equipped with sufficient resources for such an ambitious task. You will fail to provide the kind of excellent value that repeat customers seek. As a result, your business will steadily lose customers.

Top executives sit down with their senior managers to do business planning with a focus on a particular market before they take action.

BB&T, a bank that started in North Carolina, positioned itself in the market with a down-to-earth caring approach like a local bank. It launched a campaign to market its services to small businesses and made it clear that they considered every Carolina entrepreneur as a small business owner. Thus, they reinforced the idea that they are dedicated to their specific target market—the small business owner.[4]

Ford Motor Company's 1999 annual report was entitled, "Connecting with Customers," which has been Ford's focus. "A customer-driven company must be relentless in its focus. It must listen to customers, find ways to fill their needs, and continually seek feedback on how well it is satisfying those needs," the report noted. Ford has been trying to reach customers who "trust our company, love our brands, and delight in our services." In order to fulfill this goal, Ford has been using the Customer-Driven Six Sigma for quality control, which corresponds with only allowing 3.4 defects per million. The company hit tough times when the Firestone tires problem surfaced, but management vowed to refocus on the customer.[5]

Network Display, a manufacturer of point-of-purchase advertising displays, was not growing much in an industry with a five-year growth rate of 23 percent. So president Kathy Fyler took drastic measures to get rid of Network Display's least promising customers. These were the customers who took up most of Network's time and had little potential for any future growth. For the company to have the opportunity to grow, Fyler had to rethink its list of customers.

Fyler put it this way: "We decided to fire the clients that were consuming lots of time and energy with a small level of return and low potential for growth." Then Fyler went on to say, "We decided to really focus on the existing clients who had the largest potential." When Fyler had completed her list of high potential customers, she tailored the company's products to fit their particular needs. She focused on her target market and as a result Network Display's five-year growth rate was a fantastic 507 percent.[6]

Upon reaching the Gold Medal Level, a company dominates the market of a specific target group with long-term profitability. The business has somewhat of a monopoly in that market segment. When the target group is asked, your company's name comes up. In the market, you have created a special niche (a narrowly defined group which is seeking a unique mix of benefits). You are the primary firm that fulfills the needs and wants of that particular market segment. You have become the "owner" of that segment and the customers recognize and know that your company is the leader.

These companies look at marketing as a way to cultivate customer relationships. Instead of the customer feeling like an outsider, these businesses make customers feel like they are "family," individualizing and meeting their needs and wants. This contributes to their profitability in the long run. Some sterling examples of companies that have dominated their target markets are:

- Coca-Cola,
- Microsoft,
- Nike, and
- Wal-Mart.

The third largest chicken producer in the United States, Perdue Farms, has a margin that is above the industry average. In its major markets, it has reached up to 50 percent market share with its major product of chicken. It has targeted the market that is willing to pay a premium for their chickens because the birds are on a chemical-free diet. The company has created a market niche and is very successful in dominating its target market. Perdue Farm's founder, Frank Perdue, is fond of saying, "It takes a tough man to make a tender chicken."[7]

> *"I don't know the key to success, but the key to failure is to try to please everyone."*
>
> —Bill Cosby

Dynamic Twenty-Five: Focus on Your Target Market		
Score	Level	Description
☐ 1-5	Endangered Survivor Level	Everyone in the market is viewed as a potential customer.
☐ 6-10	Struggling Survivor Level	Your company tries to become a leader in all of the customer groups in your industry, and has not fully defined a specific target market.
☐ 11-15	Enduring Survivor Level	Your company has defined its target market, but has not yet determined the specific needs and wants of those target customers.

Dynamic Twenty-Five: Focus on Your Target Market		
Score	Level	Description
☐ 16-20	Bronze Medal Level	Your company has fully defined its target market by identifying which market segments can be best served by the core competencies of your company.
☐ 21-25	Silver Medal Level	Your company has not only fully defined its target market by identifying which market segments are compatible with the core competencies of your company, but it has also tailored a marketing program that effectively reaches that target market.
☐ 26-30	Gold Medal Level	Your company has made a niche in the market and dominates the market of a specific target group with long-term profitability.

Dynamic Twenty-Six

Innovate Customer Solutions

"If we stop innovating and stop bringing new electronic devices to market, we'll die."

—Mickey Schulhof, former CEO, Sony[1]

Many guests of the Lötschberg Hotel in Interlaken, Switzerland, repeatedly return for their vacations from year to year. There they receive—on a daily basis—a variety of individually tailored and innovative options for vacation activities. This traditional villa-style hotel is located in the heart of a renowned tourist center that lies between two gorgeous lakes in the Swiss Alps with views to the highest mountain peaks of Europe, including the famous Jungfrau. There, the competition among the numerous hotels is quite fierce.

What sets the Lötschberg Hotel apart from others nearby is the unique, personalized attention you will receive from Susi and Fritz Hutmacher, who own and run the place. Whether you come fully prepared with an itinerary of what you would like to do, or if you have no idea, they will lend you their helpful and timely advice. It is like having a friend or relative living in Interlaken telling you about all the places you should consider visiting—tailored exactly to your interests and to the day's weather conditions.

For one adventurous family with one member who could not ski because of a recent knee injury, Fritz helpfully suggested sledding at an uncrowded location not known to most tourists, but favored by the locals. To another couple and family interested in genuine Swiss fondue in an authentic setting, he personally arranged for and led a short mountain hike and a sled ride. It ended at an old rustic lodge run by a Swiss couple in their 70s who personally prepared the type of fondue and traditional Swiss drinks that the locals have enjoyed for generations.

One older gentleman who had recovered from triple bypass heart surgery and an operation to replace his knees had long desired to go paragliding. But he did not know how, where, or even if he could fulfill his dream, because he was physically unable to run in order to take off. Fritz personally took him up a gondola to a mountain ridge and paraglided with him, safely making his dream come true.

People often repeat the axiom, "Time is money." You will certainly save time and money if you stay at the Lötschberg Hotel. You won't need to waste time looking up appropriate activities to do, or trying to find their locations on the map. Both summer and winter weather can vary from day to day, making certain outings possible and others impossible that day. Fritz offers specific up-to-date weather reports, with a variety of options for activities suitable to the day's weather conditions. So you won't end up arriving at a favorite spot on a day that the weather has closed the attraction. Fritz wonderfully prepares you by volunteering all the pertinent information you need to have a great time.

"Every day, I try to see and talk to each guest at least once," explains Fritz. That is why he helps to prepare and serve the included breakfast each morning in that this gives him the opportunity to interact with his guests and to innovate customer solutions on the spot.

Early on, Fritz was one of the first hotels in Interlaken to provide Internet access for hotel guests. In fact, for a time, when guests of the nearby five-star hotel requested access to the Internet, that hotel sent them to the Lötschberg Hotel!

So if you are ever in Interlaken, check into the Lötschberg Hotel, and you will have an experience you will never forget.

By the way, if you get a chance to be their guest, ask Fritz how he likes his job. He will probably reply, "What job? This is a hobby." He obviously enjoys providing innovative customer solutions—arranging events that guests have interest in, and even serving as their personal guide to surrounding locations during the day and evening hours.

Customers everywhere are looking for solutions, not just mere products and services. That is why it is so important for executives to focus on serving the customers' needs and wants—otherwise the firm will, sooner or later, simply cease to exist. To provide sought-after solutions, businesses need to constantly evaluate the needs and wants of their customers, like Fritz does at the Lötschberg Hotel.

Because each and every product or service is subject to a life cycle, they need to be carefully monitored. In every life cycle, there is a time period of

- invention/launch,
- growth,
- maturing, and
- saturation.

Eventually, every life cycle comes to an end. When some products or services die, others emerge to take their place. Take for example the 8-track; it was replaced by the cassette, which later got replaced by the CD. As time goes on, products die and new ones are born. On the average, the contemporary product life cycles tend to consist of three years for products, one and a half years for services, and only six months for Internet services.

Amos R. McMullian, the chairman and CEO of the baking giant Flowers Industries, describes the place of innovation in his company:

"Good management must be able to break away from the habit of doing things the way they were done a long time ago. Habit is the enemy of innovation. Innovation is the mother of increased productivity. It is increased productivity that allows us to accomplish our company's mission."[2]

Marcian E. "Ted" Hoff was working for Intel back in the 1960's when Busicom placed an order with Intel to manufacture a set of 12 custom chips for its new calculator. Busicom specified that each chip would perform a single function. In taking charge of the project, Hoff wondered whether one chip could be a general-purpose central processor that could be programmed to perform each of the 12 functions that the individual chips were to perform. Hoff thought that one chip that could do various functions would be better by far.

For some reason, Intel let Hoff pursue his idea even though it was not exactly what the customer asked for. Hoff later made this remark about Intel's decision, "Those managers allowed me to break a cardinal rule of business: Always do what the customer wants. We didn't do what the customer wanted. We did something better."

All too often, when customers ask for a product or service, the run-of-the-mill company simply supplies that product or service. But instead, the top companies seek out the outcomes that a customer wants and then produce the products or services to meet those outcomes. Sometimes you know a much better way to provide a product or service than your customer even imagines, just as in this example at Intel. Hoff wasn't afraid of thinking outside the box and is credited with being an inventor of the microprocessor.[3]

Peter Drucker wrote, "One can use market research only on what is already in the market."[4] But, the top companies are not content to stagnate with the products and services they already have on the market. At the Gold Medal Level, your company will be a leader in your industry because it produces large quantities of innovative products/services.

Such a company continually "wows" their customers with new, creative innovative products and services. They gain an increasingly larger market share as they introduce improvements to existing products, and as they introduce new products and services. The company's business culture is one of innovation. Its employees and suppliers help it to create innovative customer solutions. Thus, a significant competitive advantage is gained over the competition.

Take, for example, mobile phone companies. They continually surpass each other with new and innovative ideas:

- ❖mobile phones that have access to the Internet,
- ❖mobile phones with one flat fee,
- ❖mobile phones that allow you to take and send pictures,
- ❖global phones,
- ❖mobile video-telephones, and
- ❖multiple phones on a single plan.

These examples illustrate how top businesses steadily "invent their business anew."

ATA Services, a company that does maintenance, repair, and rebranding of automated teller machines, is in an industry with a five-year negative growth rate of -17 percent. But somehow ATA Service's five-year growth rate was an amazing 1,167 percent. So how in the world did ATA Services manage to produce such outstanding growth in such a declining industry?

The answer is that they provide innovative customer solutions. ATA expanded its services and reach to provide a solution to a growing problem that affected the industry. This industry was highly populated with repair shops that operated locally to service automated teller machines. Mike Robson, the president of ATA Services, watched as the regional and national banks bought out local banks. This development created a problem for the banks putting together a large network of ATMs in various locations, which caused all types of servicing problems.

So Robson jumped into action to transform ATA Services into a one-stop ATM-maintenance shop. "We are not the low-price leader," Robson says. "But by packaging all of our services to replace many different vendor interactions, ATA provides maximum value for the banks at these hard-to-handle remote locations."

In this rapidly changing market, what Robson did was keep up with the changes and capitalize on the market situation by providing innovative customer solutions tailored to the newly emerging needs of the customers. This is how ATA Services managed to amass such an incredible growth rate in a declining growth industry.[5]

> *"Customers want to get more than mere products. They want to get solutions!"*
>
> —THOMAS J. NEVINS,
> Managing director of THT[6]

Dynamic Twenty-Six: Inovate Customer Solutions		
Score	Level	Description
☐ 1-5	Endangered Survivor Level	Your company operates in the market with the opinion, "What worked yesterday, must work today."
☐ 6-10	Struggling Survivor Level	Company executives realize that the product/service life cycles have tended to become shorter, so knowledge and innovation become necessary to lengthen the life cycle. Although your company has not yet taken action, it is evaluating these lifecycles and planning to make changes.
☐ 11-15	Enduring Survivor Level	Your company categorizes and screens its products and services, keeping only the best products and services in your product/service mix.

Dynamic Twenty-Six: Inovate Customer Solutions		
Score	**Level**	**Description**
☐ 16-20	Bronze Medal Level	Your products and services are developed according to the needs and wants of your target consumers. Teams have been established for product improvement.
☐ 21-25	Silver Medal Level	Your company is continually improving its existing products/services as well as introducing new business innovation. Your frontline employees effectively respond to customer needs and wants.
☐ 26-30	Gold Medal Level	Your company is a leader in your industry because it continually produces large quantities of innovative products/services that specifically serve customer needs and desires.

Dynamic Twenty-Seven

Guarantee Product/Service Quality

"Quality is exceeding customers' expectations. You will not be successful over time without it."

—Dan Bollom, CEO,
Wisconsin Public Service[1]

Consumers have come to expect high quality in products and services. But what really defines "high quality"? For one person it might be one specific feature, but for another person it might be a totally different consideration that leads them to conclude a product is "high quality." Quality is based on customer expectations. Therefore in order to guarantee the quality of your products, you must first determine what your customers think is high quality.

A goal of past quality control systems was to recognize errors or defects at their earliest stages and then eradicate them. But to the extent possible, today's quality control should help avoid errors or defects in the first place. It is much more cost effective for your company to prevent the errors or defects altogether instead of merely relying on identifying them and then eradicating them. Taking the newer *preventive approach* instead of the older *detection* and *correction approach* will ultimately pay off for your company.

Quality is not isolated to only one area of your business, such as the production process. Every employee, supplier, and distributor has an influence on the quality of your products and/or services. Instead of thinking of quality as an issue for a single department or function, start thinking of it as a company-wide goal. Your whole company needs to take part in making products and/or services that meet and exceed the expectations of your customers.

For your quality control system to be maximally effective, you will need all your employees and suppliers to buy into it and be involved. The employees and the suppliers need to understand how they affect the quality of your product or service. They need to understand that they are an important part in the whole process. Managers should hold each and every employee and supplier responsible for insuring the quality of their own work.

Quality must not be controlled, it must be produced.[2] Quality is not something that your employees or suppliers merely control, it is something that they must actively create. This is an extremely important distinction to communicate to your employees and suppliers in order to produce products and/or services of the highest quality.

It is not always the most complex solutions that are required to solve problems. Sometimes it is the simplest, most inexpensive solution that can eliminate defects. For example, Yamada Electric was having a recurring problem with the assembling of a simple push button switch that they manufactured. Although assembling these switches was very simple, the springs that had to be inserted under each on-and-off button would occasionally be left out. When customers discovered that they had received a defective switch, they would call Yamada Electric and personnel from Yamada would have to go to the customer's place of business to check every switch. This quality control problem was incurring huge costs for the company. Whenever a customer reported a defect incident, the managers would urge workers to be more careful not to forget the springs in assembly. For a while, quality would improve, but again and again the problem would resurface. This recurring problem was a thorn in Yamada's side and a constant embarrassment for its executives.

An expert in quality control, Shigeo Shingo, was hired as a consultant to solve the problem. He suggested a very simple solution. Place a small bowl next to each assembly station. Before assembling each switch, have the assembler pull out two springs and place them in the bowl. If at the end of the assembling of the switch there was a spring left in the dish, the worker would know that it was left out and the switch could be immediately reassembled. This simple, inexpensive solution eliminated the problem.[3]

Companies reaching the Gold Medal Level have such systems in place that avoid defects and errors. A total quality management program (TQM) is in place.

Once you have reached this level, there is still no time to relax. Managers must constantly be searching for potential errors and defects, and turning any discovery of such a problem into a challenge for your employees to solve. Continually interview your customers to determine their expectations. Constantly compare your company with other businesses in your industry, with the goal to be the leader with the highest quality.

Debbie Young became aware of a quality problem while working at a furniture company in Atlanta, Georgia. The company she worked for had poor quality controls that led to inconsistency in the level of quality of their products. Young became frustrated when nothing was done about the problem after she brought it to the attention of her supervisor. So she decided to leave the company and start up her own company to see if she could do better.

Young started her own company, Windham Castings, only to run into quality problems of her own. The furniture that Young had ordered from Mexico was not up to her quality standards. She decided that to be able to guarantee the quality of her products she would have to open her own permanent mold foundry, which she did in 2000.

Before building her own foundry, Young went to the Georgia Institute of Technology for some consultation. They advised her on the specific equipment to buy and how to design her plant for optimal productivity. "I didn't know anything about manufacturing," admits Young. "We had to be innovative and efficient, and we learned as we went." It is highly unusual for someone in her industry to have their own foundry, but it has paid off for Windham Castings. Young has been able to cut labor cost by 10 percent, speed up delivery, and guarantee the quality of her products. The revenues of Windham increased an amazing 60 percent from $5 million in 2000 to $8 million in 2001.

Young's dedication to quality has given her company a competitive edge and even more so after September 11, 2001, when patriotism increased, influencing more U.S. consumers to become interested in purchasing products that are "Made in America."[4]

> *"The old-style approach was to say, 'We've got great quality. We have 40 quality control inspectors in the factory.' Then somebody realized that if you need 40 inspectors, it must be a lousy factory. So now the trick is to run a factory without any quality control inspectors; each employee is his or her own quality control person."*
>
> —JOHN K. SHANK, professor, Dartmouth College[5]

Dynamic Twenty-Seven: Guarantee Product/Service Quality		
Score	Level	Description
☐ 1-5	Endangered Survivor Level	Your company determines quality. Errors and defects are removed without necessarily eradicating the source of the problem.
☐ 6-10	Struggling Survivor Level	Your company has regular quality control checks. Quality problems are solved, in part, through higher production.
☐ 11-15	Enduring Survivor Level	Every employee is responsible for the quality of his or her own work. Every defect or error is carefully analyzed to determine the cause of the problem.

Dynamic Twenty-Seven: Guarantee Product/Service Quality		
Score	Level	Description
☐ 16-20	Bronze Medal Level	Your company has established quality control teams that target recurring errors or defects and introduce solutions to correct those problems. The company has standardized the remediation of errors or defects.
☐ 21-25	Silver Medal Level	Your company has taken a preventive approach toward errors and defects. The employees are continually on the look out for ways to stop errors and defects from occurring. Your definition of high quality comes straight from your customers.
☐ 26-30	Gold Medal Level	Your company has systems in place that avoid defects and errors. There is an effective total quality management program (TQM) in place.

Dynamic Twenty-Eight

Cultivate Public Relations

"While organizations perform either good or poor public relations, public relations as a professionally directed activity has nearly always evolved after a crisis situation. In other words, the organization had to find itself in enough difficulty to recognize the need for professional assistance and guidance. Prior to that point in time, managers have normally maintained that what needs to be done in the area of public relations, they could do."

—Melvin L. Sharpe[1]

Many entrepreneurs believe that offering an exceptionally outstanding product is all that is needed to hold one's position in the market. However, this can be a fatal error. You must actively use some means of communication to stay noticed in the market. Your company must have effective two-way communication with the public.[2]

Good public relations are useful in two respects:

- Your business becomes more attractive to potential future employees.
- Your products and/or services become more accessible to customers by being presented appropriately to the target market.

Managers especially at the executive level, hold the responsibility for the public relations functions of a company. The first country to have researched and formulated a body of information on public relations was South Africa. Since that time, there has been continual growth in the field of public relations.[3]

The International Public Relations Association (IPRA) defines "public relations practice" as the "art and social science of analyzing trends, predicting their consequences, counseling the leaders of organizations and implementing planned programs of action, which will serve both the organization and the public interest."

The Public Relations Institute of Southern Africa (PRISA) adopted this definition of public relations: "Public relations is the management, through communication, of perceptions and strategic relationships between an organization and its internal and external stakeholders."[4]

The public's actual perception of the company is what is most important, not how the organization *thinks* the public perceives it. The public's perception may be rooted in facts or fiction, but both affect the public's view of the company. This is why effective public relations are required to help support and convey to the public an accurate, realistic understanding of a particular company situation.[5]

The size of your company will influence whether you employ an editor of a student newspaper (for example) or a public relations professional. In any case, it is important to use the media for your own benefit. For establishing positive public attention on your business, you need to have a standardized and unique public presentation—that is, a corporate design.

One day while Jon Stocking was fishing on a boat out in the middle of the Pacific Ocean, he had the opportunity to save a dolphin from the fisherman's nets. That experience opened Stocking's eyes and he decided from that day forth that he would take some sort of environmental action daily.

Soon, he decided to start Endangered Species Chocolate Company. "I thought chocolate would be a great medium for an environmental message—to use the product as a vehicle to educate and donate," says Stocking. He started his company in 1994 in Talent, Oregon, and his sales have soared to over $2 million per year.[6]

Stocking features endangered species on his candy bars and he donates 10 percent of profits to saving those particular endangered species such as cheetahs, sea otters, sea turtles, orangutans, and others. Some of the contributions go directly to organizations like Wildlife Conservation Society, Jane Goodall Institute, and Defenders of Wildlife, to name a few. Stocking's environmental involvement in helping save endangered species has given him huge amounts of positive public relations, which helps his company thrive.

At the Gold Medal Level, a company's well-developed media contacts result in positive press coverage of all business activities. The corporate public image matches how the corporation in reality functions. The International Public Relations Code of Ethics is followed. Both the organization and the public interest are served.

Media representatives and befriended journalists are regularly invited for background interviews. In this way, they are always kept informed about all the latest important developments. Subsequently, the media report frequently about the business. The carefully created corporate design concept exists not only on paper, but is internalized and implemented by every employee on a daily basis in every area.

> *"A good name is more desirable than great riches; to be esteemed is better than silver or gold."*[7]

Dynamic Twenty-Eight: Cultivate Public Relations		
Score	**Level**	**Description**
☐ 1-5	Endangered Survivor Level	The company has no public relations, or has poor public relations.
☐ 6-10	Struggling Survivor Level	Company executives have thought about public relations and have chosen to stay out of the media if at all possible.
☐ 11-15	Enduring Survivor Level	Some positive public relations efforts are being made, but the majority of the available public relations techniques are not in place.

Dynamic Twenty-Eight: Cultivate Public Relations		
Score	Level	Description
☐ 16-20	Bronze Medal Level	Your company has used one of the effective techniques of public relations and has received positive media publicity.
☐ 21-25	Silver Medal Level	You have one or more public relations professionals or consultants who are separate from the marketing department. Your company has thereby received positive coverage in the media.
☐ 26-30	Gold Medal Level	The well-developed media contacts of your company result in positive press coverage of your business activities. The corporate public image matches how the corporation in reality functions. The IPR Code of Ethics is followed. Both the organization and the public interest are well served.

GOAL SIX:

ATTRACT CUSTOMER FANS

Dynamic Twenty-Nine

Provide the Best Service Quality

"Focus only on the customer, and everything else falls into its proper perspective and proper priority almost automatically."

—Robert J. Eaton, former Chrysler Chairman[1]

The customer may be compared to a full suitcase of money. Only the right combination will open the lock for you.

You cannot profit by whining and complaining about having too few customers. Invest your time and energy instead on finding the "right combination." Business success depends on everything you provide that causes customers to buy from you, causes them to come back for repeat business time and again, and causes them to recommend your company to others. The ideal combination is nurturing "customer fans." Developing "customer fans" involves marketing, sales, and customer service.

The Venetia Hotel in California is a shining example of a company that continually exceeds and excites its customer with the best service. In the lobby of the hotel there is fresh fruit, comfortable sofas, and a crackling fire that provide the ambience of a cozy home. As you register, you fill out a short survey that asks you your preferences. Once you finish registering, the bellboy promptly ushers you to your room where everything is in impeccable order. The receptionist has already set up your reservation in the adjacent restaurant, so when you arrive you are immediately shown to your table. Once you return to your room, the quilt is turned down on the bed and a mint lies on each pillow. A fire crackles in the fireplace. In the morning, the coffee pot turns on by an automatic timer so your favorite brand of coffee is brewing. Your favorite newspaper is at the door. Every time you come back to Venetia Hotel, the experience is the same. Customers leave with a warm feeling and the very pleasant memory of being "wowed" by Venetia's impeccable service.[2]

As markets get more competitive, it becomes more and more crucial that you differentiate yourself from your competition. As products and services of different companies become more and more alike, they become exchangeable by the customer base. You must somehow distinguish yourself in your customer's mind. Providing the absolute best service in your industry is one powerful way to differentiate your brand to gain a competitive edge.

Service quality can noticeably set your company apart from the pack. High quality service is often the key reason why customers buy from one company over another. Many customers are willing to pay more to get the service that they want. For many businesses, customers place less emphasis on price as they become more concerned about service quality.

Service takes place before, during and after a sale. Customers make evaluations from their preconceived notions of how they expect the service to be. For example, at a five star hotel, customers typically expect that they will have valet parking. If a customer's preconceived notions about a hotel's services do not match up with the actual performance, then that customer will be greatly disappointed. If that hotel did not provide valet parking, it would make such a bad impression that the customer would most likely never return. Even worse for the hotel, that customer is likely to spread the word about how bad that hotel's service is.

Certainly, your company doesn't want to get into this kind of downward spiral with your customer base! Consider a similar problem at a physician's office. Inadequate parking and long periods of waiting in the waiting room with only out-dated, well-worn magazines to read make it abundantly clear that the focus is not on customer-friendly service. Even in a sellers' market (as is the case with physician services), competing distributors may take your customers from you if they offer more helpful service. And for businesses not operating in a sellers' market, the lack of good service can rapidly threaten a company's very survival. If a company does not care about its customers, the competitors surely will.

At the Gold Medal Level, a company's customer service continually surprises and exceeds its customers' expectations, creating strong customer enthusiasm and loyalty. The company's positive reputation spreads like wildfire, rapidly increasing your market share and clearly distinguishing it as the best.

When you are successful in repeatedly exceeding the expectations of your customers, your customers become your "fans." Your company is known for its excellent personalized customer service. You maintain high standards for service. Unexpected services make your customers feel exceptionally cared-for and extremely pleased with the outcome. Your company "wows" your customers again and again, continually meeting their needs and desires in pleasantly surprising ways.

Your service can be compared to a house: the foundation is the company's mission; the building structure represents the business itself. The fixtures, interior, and outside landscaping of the house represent the personalized professional services that create the "wow" experience.

Chuck Bond, owner and founder of COKEM International, has seen his company's sales boom from $17 million in 2000, to $77 million in 2001. What is Bond's secret recipe for success?

Bond's foundation is a set of strong ethical values such as honesty, fairness, and promptly following through on commitments. These values undergird and empower his central focus which he described this way:

"Service is definitely the key to our success. If you service at a higher-than-expected level, you usually outperform the competition." COKEM keeps a close watch on their retail customers' inventories, and continually packages and provides better products to fit the needs of each customer. This service gives COKEM a heads up over their competition. Bond's company has been able to capture business from retail giants such as Best Buy, Target, Sam's Club, and Office Depot. Clearly, Bond's service quality is what has bolstered his incredible success.[3]

> *"The position a person occupies in the world depends on the quantity and the quality of the service he renders plus the mental attitude which he relates to others."*
>
> —Andrew Carnegie[4]

Dynamic Twenty-Nine: Provide the Best Service Quality		
Score	**Level**	**Description**
☐ 1-5	Endangered Survivor Level	Your company provides minimal or no customer service, perhaps because the product or service is believed to sell itself.
☐ 6-10	Struggling Survivor Level	Your company recognizes the need for customer service. It has started to differentiate itself by providing some customer service when it is requested.
☐ 11-15	Enduring Survivor Level	Your company has identified your most important customer services and has developed goals and action plans to realize those goals. The company has implemented most of these business services for customers.

Dynamic Twenty-Nine: Provide the Best Service Quality		
Score	**Level**	**Description**
☐ 16-20	Bronze Medal Level	Your high quality professionalism in customer service (friendliness, courtesy, kindness, integrity, fairness, etc.) is beginning to differentiate your company from your competitors. Your employees reliably provide this professional quality service. This service is beginning to give your company a competitive advantage.
☐ 21-25	Silver Medal Level	Your company provides excellent reliable, highly professional customer service that is widely recognized among your customer base as clearly differentiating your company from your competitors. Your superior reputation for providing the highest quality customer service contributes to your large market share.
☐ 26-30	Gold Medal Level	The customer service of your company continually surprises and exceeds the expectations of your customers, creating "customer fans" with strong customer enthusiasm and loyalty. Your positive reputation spreads like wildfire, rapidly increasing your market share and clearly distinguishing your company as the best.

Dynamic Thirty

Sell Your Strengths

"The successful salesperson cares first for the customer, second for the products."

—Philip Kotler[1]

Companies in the United States spend over a trillion dollars annually on sales force and sales force materials. Both nonprofit as well as for-profit organizations use sales forces. This is the number one promotional method used by companies today.[2]

Your salesperson or persons are windows to your company. Because salespeople directly relate to your customers, they are often the ones who ultimately convey to the customers what your business is all about. The impression they make on your potential customers ultimately reflects on your company. This makes it highly important to regularly receive feedback from those customers to evaluate your sales force. You need to make sure that your salespeople effectively communicate how your company's strengths can provide solutions needed by potential customers.

If "a chain is only as strong as its weakest link," then your company cannot be any stronger than your sales force. Your salespersons must be skilled in listening to potential customers to assess their needs. The most highly successful salespeople focus on the needs and wants of your customers. Your sales force must not only sell your company's products or services as solutions to customer needs, but also be adept at selling themselves as well. That is, they must develop attractive ongoing relationships with customers because those relationships can help make or break repeat sales.

But at the highest level—the Gold Medal Level, not only does your sales department bring in sales, but other employees in other departments also make sales by how they too relate to customers. Every one of your employees feels like a representative of your business and tries to obtain orders for your business. Employees are motivated to gain sales orders because they are specifically rewarded for doing so by your company policy. This is one way that your company fulfills the needs of your customers so well that they become "fans" and tell others about what you have to offer.

When a customer receives a product or service and it exceeds their expectations, they are naturally prone to tell others about it. This is how I found my barber Buddy at The Rouge Haircutters in West Columbia, South Carolina. A friend referred my father to The Rouge around eleven years ago. Dad was so pleased with his haircut and the prompt service from Buddy that he referred my four brothers and me to Buddy. All five of us brothers started getting our hair cut by Buddy and we too were quite pleased with Buddy's hair cutting expertise, his meticulous following of our instructions, and the way he conversed with us while trimming our hair. And so for many years now, my four brothers and I have had our hair cut by only one barber—Buddy—and it would be quite accurate to call us his customer "fans."

So—as "fans" are prone to do—all five of us started telling our friends about how Buddy cuts our hair exactly the way we want it. We emphasized that he carefully takes the extra time to listen to what each particular customer wants. Many of our friends also began getting their haircuts from Buddy. This chain of spontaneous referrals to Buddy by his "fans" was made possible by Buddy's strengths in providing top-notch service in a very friendly way.

Note too, that among the several employees at The Rouge Haircutters, Buddy is not even formally assigned any specific duties to sell the services and products of the company; that responsibility lies with the main co-owners of the store. Although Buddy is just another barber in the store, he too makes sales by how he relates to and serves the company's customers. At The Rouge, Buddy is thereby involved in selling the strengths of the company.

When customers become your "fans," they become your most important salespeople. Your company's reputation grows and both existing and new customers continually promote your business by spontaneously referring other consumers your way.

> *"Marketing is far too important to be left only to the marketing department!"*
>
> —DAVID PACKARD, Hewlett-Packard[3]

Dynamic Thirty: Sell Your Strengths		
Score	**Level**	**Description**
☐ 1-5	Endangered Survivor Level	Your company does not have a sales force or any systematic way of generating sales. Management has never formally assessed how customers are acquired or what their specific needs are.
☐ 6-10	Struggling Survivor Level	The sales department handles the full responsibility of generating sales at your company. There is a growing awareness of the need to discover the needs of your potential customers.
☐ 11-15	Enduring Survivor Level	The sales of your company are the joint responsibility of your sales department and managers. Some of these employees are beginning to gather information on the needs of potential customers.

Dynamic Thirty: Sell Your Strengths		
Score	**Level**	**Description**
☐ 16-20	Bronze Medal Level	Your company has a well-trained sales force and a customer-involved management who periodically seek feedback on customer needs. All your employees are supporters of the sale.
☐ 21-25	Silver Medal Level	Your company is truly centered on your customers, and customer needs are continually assessed. All employees have a positive direct access to helping customers, in addition to your well-organized and well-trained sales force and managers.
☐ 26-30	Gold Medal Level	The existing and emerging needs of potential customers are closely monitored and communicated to all employees to better serve them. Not only does your sales department bring in sales, but sales are also made by employees in many different departments. Your customers become "fans" because your company is so attentive to their needs, and they too, bring in more customers.

DYNAMIC THIRTY-ONE

DETERMINE CUSTOMER CONTENTMENT

"A good agreement is self-enforcing because both parties go away smiling and happy to see that each of us is smiling. If one smiles and the other scowls, the agreement will not stick, lawyers or no lawyers."

—CHARLES HANDY explains the "Chinese Contract"[1]

What makes your customers happy? This is one of the most important questions your company could ask. There are many benefits to keeping your customers happy. Your happy customers tend to

- ❖spend more money,
- ❖buy more products and use more services,
- ❖buy more frequently,

- ❖be less price sensitive, and
- ❖promote your company as customer "fans" who are highly loyal to your company.

All these benefits point to the necessity of evaluating how your customers think about your company's performance. In a competitive market, a significant way to sustain a competitive edge over your competition is to continually make your customers happy. But, in order to do this, your company must determine exactly what it is that makes your particular customers happy.

Our favorite book of wisdom, the Bible, gives this advice: "Each of you should look not only to your own interests, but also to the interests of others."[2] If we follow this sound advice, we will want to learn more about the interests of our customers so we can serve them well.

One of the keys to business success is to provide products and/or services that meet the needs and wants of your customers. That is, your company must look out for the interests of your customers. And how do you look out for your customer's interest if you don't know what they are? You can't! That's why it is imperative that you listen carefully to your customers to discover their ongoing expectations. To develop customers who become "fans" of your company, you must collect some kind of data to know how to meet and exceed their expectations with your products and/or services.

There are many different ways that you and your employees can discover what it is about your products or services that makes customers happy and to discover what changes you can introduce to make them even happier. Armed with this vital information, you can develop or enhance the features or benefits that you offer to your customers. Also, if you learn that your customers consider some specific features of your products or services undesirable, you know exactly what to change to better please them.

Your employees should be trained to be constantly on the look out for anything that makes the customer happy or unhappy. For example, if your salesperson says something that results in a customer's facial expression of disapproval, the salesperson should pick up on it and explore the root of such discontent. Then they should let you, the management, know about it so you can take appropriate action.

Your employees can learn many observational techniques of gathering information from your customers. For example, many grocery chains and retail stores offer their regular customers a member discount card. This card gathers information on each individual customer's buying pattern, thus helping the company market directly and more effectively to that particular customer.

At the Gold Medal Level, a company emphasizes dialogue with customers in order to stay current on what makes them maximally satisfied. The firm keeps an extensive database on its customers, detailing important information about their buying patterns in order to meet and exceed their expectations.

By implementing a well-tuned database system, your business has access to a large amount of information on specific customers. This enables your company to tailor its products and/or services to the specific needs and wants of each customer. When the database information is used to increase the satisfaction of each customer, they get the impression that they are most important.

Some people might say that Rick Skidmore's Timberlane Woodcrafters, which manufactures wooden shutters, is part of an industry with little potential growth. And if you were to look at the industry's five-year growth rate of only 3 percent, you would agree. So how did Timberlane Woodcrafters manage to grow 758 percent in five years?

Skidmore relentlessly pursued customers for referrals and obtained customer feedback on their contentment with Timberlane Woodcrafters' products. Most of Timberlane's customers bought wooden shutters only once from the company. So Skidmore did his best to impress his customers in hopes of motivating them to refer their friends to him. The plan worked and referrals to the company increased 5 percent each year, amounting to 25 percent of the company's overall sales.

Skidmore actively assesses customer contentment. When a customer is dissatisfied with the product, the company immediately gets in touch with that customer to promise and then deliver a quick resolution. The company recently adopted a practice of sending the dissatisfied customer an "Oops Kit" that contains a flashlight and a little note that thanks the customer for "shedding light on the mistake."

While Timberlane strives to provide the highest quality products to its customers, Skidmore believes that providing superior service makes even the occasional unhappy customer become the company's biggest fan. Skidmore's extra effort to seek out referrals and make sure that his customers are happy has made Timberlane successful even in a low growth industry.[3]

> *"Your most unhappy customers are your greatest source of learning."*
>
> —BILL GATES

Dynamic Thirty-One: Determine Customer Contentment		
Score	Level	Description
☐ 1-5	Endangered Survivor Level	Your company collects no data on what satisfies your customers.
☐ 6-10	Struggling Survivor Level	Your managers and employees do view customer satisfaction as important, but no action has been taken beyond employee discussions about how customers might feel and how to measure customer reactions to your products and/or services.
☐ 11-15	Enduring Survivor Level	A small portion of your customers (such as your most important or most frequent or most recent customers) are evaluated with regard to customer service and are found to be usually satisfied.

Dynamic Thirty-One: Determine Customer Contentment		
Score	**Level**	**Description**
☐ 16-20	Bronze Medal Level	Your company assesses the satisfaction of your customers in a systematic way once a year, and has implemented improvements that have increased satisfaction.
☐ 21-25	Silver Medal Level	Your company operates on the premise that the "customer is boss." Employees are involved in proposing improvements designed to increase customer satisfaction in response to data collected from customers several times a year.
☐ 26-30	Gold Medal Level	Your company emphasizes continual dialogue with numerous customers in order to stay current on what makes them maximally satisfied. Also you keep an extensive database of your customers, detailing important information about their buying habits that you use to meet and exceed their expectations.

Dynamic Thirty-Two

Increase Your Delivery Performance

"Time is money."

—Benjamin Franklin

A Mexican restaurant called Monterrey's has made delivery performance a core competence. Although Monterrey's is not a fast-food restaurant, it delivers its food very fast. Right when you enter the doors of the restaurant, a greeter promptly seats you. Immediately after you sit down at your table, chips, salsa, and a glass of water are served. Your order is promptly taken and your food arrives very quickly. Monterrey's consistently delivers quickly and is widely known by local customers for their exceptional speed and consistency. In fact, when potential customers are short on time for a business lunch or dinner but prefer not to dine at an ordinary fast food establishment, Monterrey's

Restaurant rapidly comes to mind as a viable option. This reliable, extraordinarily rapid service has allowed Monterrey's to have quicker turnover than other restaurants and thereby maximizes their profits as well as their positive reputation.

Clearly, in today's marketplace, your delivery performance needs to meet or exceed the expectations of your customers. As more and more customers have pushed for better service, rapid delivery has become increasingly expected. If your company does not deliver in a trustworthy manner and on time, you will soon lose your customers to your competitors who deliver promptly and more reliably. Furthermore, many customers are willing to pay more for products and services if they are served better and more quickly.

Reducing your inventory and increasing delivery performance are two challenges that every business faces. If your company uses a "just-in-time" system, your ability to make prompt delivery will not be possible unless your suppliers deliver to you reliably. In order to stay competitive in your industry, your company must constantly develop efficient in-house procedures and supplier processes to improve your delivery performance. Top companies have done so and turned rapid delivery performance into a competitive advantage.

At the Gold Medal Level, your company's delivery performance is so good that it has become one of your core competencies, thereby giving you a strong competitive advantage. Your company has an automatic Kanban system in place. Your suppliers and departments reliably deliver "just-in-time" so you are able to cut your inventory and run more effectively and efficiently, eliminating waste and allowing you to focus labor and resources on delivery speed and high quality. Your company has implemented a system that rewards employees and your suppliers whose performance contribute to 100 percent on-time deliveries. Your customers are excited about your company because their expectations of delivery were exceeded.

> *"The early bird gets the worm, but the second mouse gets the cheese."*
>
> —Author Unknown

Dynamic Thirty-Two: Increase Your Delivery Performance		
Score	**Level**	**Description**
☐ 1-5	Endangered Survivor Level	The products or services of your company are frequently delivered later than promised due to inefficiencies such as lack of components from your suppliers, wasted time trying to locate products in an unorganized inventory, or items being out of stock due to lack of planning.
☐ 6-10	Struggling Survivor Level	Your company assesses and identifies causes of poor delivery performance. However, no corrective action has yet been taken to eliminate the source of the delivery problems.
☐ 11-15	Enduring Survivor Level	Your company has corrected some past managerial and procedural inefficiencies causing problems in your delivery performance. Bottlenecks in your processes are identified and worked on. Regular meetings are held to discuss the progress of all the customer orders, and to proactively monitor and prevent late deliveries. Thus, on time delivery performance has substantially improved.

Dynamic Thirty-Two: Increase Your Delivery Performance		
Score	**Level**	**Description**
☐ 16-20	Bronze Medal Level	Your company measures and sets high goals for your delivery performance. Employees report early indications of an impending late delivery to managers. Thus, the customer is informed ahead of time (or the delivery dates of the other customers for the same product might be able to be re-negotiated with discounts) in order to deliver on time to the customer needing more urgent delivery.
☐ 21-25	Silver Medal Level	Your company has control systems in place that regulate the efficiency and speed of your processes responsible for delivery performance. You have negotiated shared responsibilities with your suppliers and actively obtain feedback from your customers on delivery issues. You are among the best in your industry for on-time deliveries.
☐ 26-30	Gold Medal Level	Your delivery performance is so good that it has become one of your core competencies, thereby giving you a strong competitive advantage. Your company has an automatic Kanban system in place. Your workstations and suppliers reliably perform and deliver "just-in-time." Consistent employee and supplier motivation is achieved by a reward system for prompt employee performance associated with on-time delivery.

Dynamic Thirty-Three

Nurture Customer Relationships

"My business absolute is delighting the customer."
—Shelly Carpenter, human resources director, Johnson & Johnson[1]

Johnson & Johnson discovered a secret to success—nurturing customer relationships.

As business competition has intensified and the array of products and services has exploded in number, it has become increasingly important to nurture positive relationships with your customers. The goal is to develop enthusiastic and useful relationships with your customers, causing them to be so excited about what you offer that they automatically buy from your company. High quality personal contact with your customers helps to achieve this.

Positive relationships with your customers should be at the top of your company's priorities and central to your focus. Like all other relationships, developing excellent customer relationships usually requires spending time with them. Try to determine their needs and wants. Keep a pulse on their every expectation of you.

The more you nurture your customer relationships, the greater the opportunity for your company to be profitable in the long run. Delight your customers. Then they will repay you with their repeat business.

Dr. Richard Yung makes an effort to build cordial relationships with every one of his dental patients. Before beginning every checkup, he chats with the patient to get to know them better. Dr. Yung performs every checkup himself rather than delegate the job to a dental assistant. His personal touch helps him develop customer "fans" who keep returning and who promote his business by referring their friends. If you are one of Dr. Yung's patients, you will most definitely receive a birthday card in the mail from him right on time. Dr. Yung is a model for the cultivation of the highly positive relationships with his customers.

Custom Solutions International, an environmental consulting and construction services company, has a whopping growth rate of 635 percent over a five-year period while the industry rate is only 17 percent. How did Custom Solutions grow so much?

Bill Baugh, CEO of Custom Solutions, believes in keeping things personal. He believes in keeping in constant contact with customers. He knows that building fruitful customer relationships requires spending the extra time with the customer. "We try to get in front of prospective clients as soon and as often as possible," says Baugh.

Baugh expects that annual sales should increase from between $50,000 to $75,000 from each customer that he visits most frequently within the next five years. "My personal record is eight trips to an office that is over a hundred miles away," explains Mr. Baugh. Baugh's personal touch ultimately pays off in the long run, building profitable customer relationships that last.[2]

At the Gold Medal Level, your company continually exceeds your customers' expectations. Your relationships with your customers are so outstanding that they have become enthusiastic "fans" of your company, bringing in new customers. In a sense, they become your best salespeople.

Often, a reward system is introduced to reward existing customers who bring in new customers.

Executives at the Gold Medal Level often use "value-based customer segmentation," a method in which they segment their customers based on their value to the company. Then they allocate greater resources to retain and increase the number of the most profitable and most loyal customers. Thus, changing providers does not even cross the mind of their customers. The customer feels like he or she is highly valued and sticks with your company through thick and thin.

In giving an answer to an expert in the law, Jesus stated that one of the two greatest commandments is: "Love your neighbor as yourself."[3] But wanting to justify himself, the expert in the law asked this Great Teacher, "And who is my neighbor?"[4] The Great Teacher answered with a story:

> "A man was going down from Jerusalem to Jericho, when he fell into the hands of robbers. They stripped him of his clothes, beat him and went away, leaving him half dead. A priest happened to be going down the same road, and when he saw the man, he passed by on the other side. So too, a Levite, when he came to the place and saw him, passed by on the other side. But a Samaritan, as he traveled, came where the man was; and when he saw him, he took pity on him. He went to him and bandaged his wounds, pouring on oil and wine. Then he put the man on his own donkey, took him to an inn and took care of him. The next day he took out two silver coins and gave them to the innkeeper. 'Look after him,' he said, 'and when I return, I will reimburse you for any extra expense you may have.'" "Which of these three do you think was a neighbor to the man who fell into the hands of robbers?" The expert in the law replied, "The one who had mercy on him."[5] Then the Great Teacher told the expert in the law, "Go and do likewise."[6]

If we love our customer as ourselves, we will nurture and cultivate them in the ways we ourselves would want to be treated. If you were robbed, beaten, and left lying on the side of the road, wouldn't you want someone like the Good Samaritan to come by and take care of your every need? It would be reasonable to assume that the man who was robbed became an enthusiastic "fan" of that Samaritan who helped him.

If we creatively apply this very ancient command, "Love your neighbor as yourself" to our customer service, our customers will be much more likely to become our "fans."

The retail giant Nordstrom targets its customers in a very personal way: "Dear Mrs., or Mr.— We have received our new summer collection. The collection holds items in your size, and even in your favorite color blue. We have held onto some shirts and pants that would fit your style and in your size for your convenient approval." This type of superior customer relationship melts away the competition. It is said that when a new Nordstrom store is announced to open, a retailer in the area closes down. The way Nordstrom nurtures its customer relationships gives it a powerful advantage over its competition.

> *"A company must serve a great need, perform a great service, not for owners but for customers. When it turns its back on the customer, it ceases to be profitable. It ceases to exist."*
>
> —Thomas J. Nevins,
> Managing director, THT[7]

Dynamic Thirty-Three: Nurture Customer Relationships		
Score	**Level**	**Description**
☐ 1-5	Endangered Survivor Level	Your company does not focus on nurturing customer relationships.
☐ 6-10	Struggling Survivor Level	Your company initiates contacts with customers, but only in an attempt to persuade them to make a purchase.
☐ 11-15	Enduring Survivor Level	Your company develops customer relationships, but only through a few systematic activities.

Dynamic Thirty-Three: Nurture Customer Relationships		
Score	**Level**	**Description**
☐ 16-20	Bronze Medal Level	Your company regularly contacts customers, develops effective marketing campaigns to reach targeted customers, and increases its sales as a result.
☐ 21-25	Silver Medal Level	Your customers view their relationship with you as a win-win relationship characterized by fulfilling their own needs and increasing the sales of your company at the same time. Your products and/or services have clearly-defined and well-communicated benefits that win over your customers.
☐ 26-30	Gold Medal Level	Your company continually exceeds the expectations of your customers. Your relationships with your customers are so outstanding that they have become enthusiastic "fans" of your company who bring in new customers. Through value-based customer segmentation, you allocate greater resources to retain and increase the number of the most profitable and most loyal customers.

EPILOGUE

TAKE ACTION TO GET TO THE TOP

"Innovation is at once the creator and destroyer of industries and corporations. Over the years, new technologies have made industrial giants out of many upstart firms, invigorated older ones that were receptive to change, and swept away those that were not. Today, when competitiveness hinges on the ability to develop or adapt new technologies in products, services, and processes, understanding the dynamics of industrial innovation and change is essential for survival and success."

—JAMES UTTERBACK,
Sloan Graduate School of Management,
Massachusetts Institute of Technology[1]

Just imagine yourself with extraordinary managerial insight and competence, dynamically leading your company to the very top of your industry, up to the very point of market dominance. Wouldn't that be great?

Although genuinely desiring to reach the top, all to often managers simply do not lead with the kind of systematic action necessary to achieve excellence. Many managers and owners only "dream" about being number one in their industry. They momentarily think about operating more effectively, but then hurriedly base crucial day-to-day management decisions on "seat-of-the-pants" guessing.

The above quote by James Utterback at M.I.T. indicates why a company's very survival and success hinge on mastering "the *dynamics* of...innovation and change." To stay in the competition, managers must vigorously condition themselves for the Olympic-level performance that is demanded by these dynamics of change. When executives fail to understand these dynamics, their companies face massive failure in the fiercest competition. So the very best managers reach for nothing less than a Gold Medal Level performance.

It's not by pure accident that some managers propel themselves to the top executive ranks and then lead their companies to excel. How do they do it?

Exceptionally outstanding managers study the *dynamic action steps* taken by the most effective companies. Then they custom design their own similar executive action steps for strategic leadership in their own company. In fact, more often than not, those same star managers landed promotions to CEO because of their Gold Medal Level performance in creatively implementing benchmarked best practices when they were still middle managers.

Calculate Your Total Score

If you have rated your company on all 33 dynamics with the self-rating tools at the end of each chapter, you can now plot your scores on the 33Dynamics Profile chart and then calculate your *Total Score.* On the next two pages you will see the Profile chart. Enter your score for each individual dynamic along the very bottom row of the Profile. Then plot your scores on the 33Dynamics Profile. Now you can simply add up the 33 scores and place the total in the box below "Total." To determine your *Overall Company Classification,* plot your *Total Score* under the "Overall" section on the far right hand side of the 33Dynamics Profile. This identifies your overall company level.

	Goal One	Goal Two	Goal Three
35			
Platinum Level			
30			
Gold Medal Level			
25			
Silver Medal Level			
20			
Bronze Medal Level			
15			
Enduring Survivor Level			
10			
Struggling Survivor Level			
5			
Endangered Survivor Level			
0			
Dynamic #	1 2 3 4 5 6	7 8 9 10 11 12	13 14 15 16 17 18
Scores			

GOAL FOUR	GOAL FIVE	GOAL SIX	OVERALL
			990
			857
			692
			527
			362
			197
			0
19 20 21 22 23	24 25 26 27 28	29 30 31 32 33	TOTAL

Now Take Action!

If you have completed the 33Dynamics Profile, congratulations! This Profile provides you a snapshot of the strengths and weaknesses of your company, based on your self-rating. Now you are poised to take decisive executive action to strategically improve your firm's management.

You will recall from an earlier section in this book that Microsoft founder, Bill Gates, confided to a TV interviewer that if he fell asleep for half a year, he would wake up to find Microsoft way behind the competition. Why? Because today, all successful business must be *dynamic*—that is, continually adapting to rapid change with highly competitive excellence.

We have pointed out that globalization of markets and rapid technological change create a harsh reality: The company that stands still in a static stance will struggle to survive.

You must continually improve your processes, your products, your customer service, your information technology, etc. You must carefully position yourself to maintain a competitive advantage. In this sense, there is no time to take a nap or to slow down.

Executives of top performing companies clearly distinguish themselves from the rest of the pack by relentlessly pursuing these overarching goals for excellence:

- ❖maximizing company performance,
- ❖managing effectively through servant leadership,
- ❖creating a superior workforce,
- ❖providing a work environment that produces loyal employees,
- ❖achieving market dominance, and
- ❖nurturing customer fans.

In all the 33 dynamics of management needed to achieve these six overarching goals, the most highly effective executives push their company's performance to a Bronze Medal Level, then the Silver Medal, and finally cross the finish line to win the coveted Gold Medal. This top-level executive performance maximizes profits for shareholders.

Two keys can open the door to such top-level performance. Equipped with these keys, executives can lead their company right to the top of their industry:

Key #1

Compare your company to the Gold Medal Levels of the 33 dynamics of managerial excellence practiced by the world's top companies. You already have this key in your hand if you have just now completed reading this book, and if you have rated your own company on each dynamic with the rating forms provided at the end of each chapter. If you think your company could increase its effectiveness and profitability through moving to higher levels on some or all of these 33 dynamics, consider this: Why not arrange for your company to order a copy of this book for all your employees so you can all be "on the same page." As management focuses on a particular dynamic, all your employees can be challenged to read that chapter and then participate in collaborative goal-setting and strategic planning in that area. (You can order more copies of this book at www.33dynamics.com).

Key #2

Work towards implementing Gold Medal Level performance for all 33 Dynamics in your company by customizing the clearly defined *Dynamic Action Steps* that have propelled the world's top companies to heights of competitive excellence. The *33Dynamics™ seminar, coaching,* and *consulting services* are designed to provide you with this second key to becoming a top-performing executive. These services offer over 500 specific Dynamic Action Steps that the leading companies currently practice. Our seminar, coaching, and consulting services can help you select from these 500+ Dynamic Action Steps and then customize them to your own company in order to move up to higher levels for each of the 33Dynamics. These services can enhance your potential to lead your company ultimately all the way to the top of your industry.

33Dynamics™ LLC, offers you the customized services of highly qualified and experienced business leaders. Our seminar leaders, executive coaches, and consultants not only hold earned M.B.A. and doctoral degrees in executive management, accounting, finance, marketing, psychology, organizational behavior, or human resource management, but they also possess the practical wisdom gained from years of corporate management experience themselves.

Now that you hold key #1 in your hand, you are ready to obtain key #2 to unlock vital resources to guide you to the top in executive management! Our website at www.33dynamics.com is designed to help you tap into the seminar, coaching, and/or consulting services that you can use to head for the top.

A Far-reaching Vision

In addition to helping U.S. companies, 33Dynamics LLC has dedicated significant amounts of its profits to helping orphans and abandoned street children around the world. We plan to expand our past charitable efforts to provide them not only with food and shelter, but we will also teach them these productive business principles to equip them to support themselves and their families when they grow up. A strategic part of our vision is to inspire others who are moving up to the top to similarly share their business expertise and profits with tragically disadvantaged children around the world. We hope to inspire other successful business persons to discover that the greatest satisfaction of generating wealth is to lovingly share it with the disadvantaged who cannot yet help themselves.

> *"If you give the poor a fish, they will eat for a day; but if you teach them how to fish, they will eat for a lifetime."*
>
> —Chinese Proverb (paraphrased)

Bibliography

Barker, Emily. "Red-tape brainstorms," The Inc 500 America's Fastest-Growing Private Companies, *INC Magazine*, October 15, 2000.

Bateman, Thomas S., & Snell, Scott A. *Management: Competing in the New Era, Fifth Edition*. Boston: McGraw-Hill Irwin, 2002.

Baye, Michael R. *Managerial Economics & Business Strategy, Third Edition*. Boston: McGraw-Hill Irwin, 2000.

Beatty, Richard H., & Burkholder, Nicholas C. *The Executive Career Guide for MBAs: Inside Advice on Getting to the Top from Today's Business Leaders*. New York: John Wiley & Sons, 1996.

Beckett, John D. *Loving Monday: Succeeding in Business Without Selling Your Soul*. Downers Grove, Illinois: InterVarsity Press, 1998.

Bennis, W., & Nanus, B. *Leaders*. New York: Harper & Row, 1985.

Blanchard, Kenneth, & Johnson, Spencer. *The One Minute Manager*. La Jolla, CA: Blanchard Johnson Publishers, 1981.

Bogan, Christopher E., & English, Michael J. *Benchmarking for Best Practices: Winning Through Innovative Adaptation*. New York: McGraw-Hill, 1994.

Camp, Robert C. *Business Process Benchmarking: Finding and Implementing Best Practices*. Milwaukee, Wisconsin: ASQC Quality Press, 1995.

Carr, Albert Z. "Is business bluffing ethical?" *Harvard Business Review, 46*, January-February 1968.

Chase, Richard B., Aquilano, Nicholas J., & Jacobs, F. Robert. *Operations Management for Competitive Advantage, Ninth Edition*. New York: McGraw Hill Irwin, 2001.

Clarke, Caroline V. *Take a Lesson: Today's Black Achievers on How They Made It & What They Learned Along the Way*. New York: John Wiley & Sons, 2001.

Collins, James C., & Porras, Jerry I. *Built to Last: Successful Habits of Visionary Companies.* New York: HarperBusiness, 1994, 1997, 2002.

Collins, Jim. *Good to Great: Why Some Companies Make the Leap...and Others Don't.* New York: HarperBusiness, 2001.

Deming, Edward W. *Out of the Crisis.* Cambridge, MA: MIT Press, 1986.

Deresky, Helen. *International Management: Managing Across Borders and Cultures.* New Jersey: Upper Saddle River, 2003.

DesJardins, Joseph R. "Virtues and business ethics," in William H. Shaw & Vincent Barry, *Moral Issues in Business, Eighth Edition.* Belmont, CA: Wadsworth Thomas Learning, 2001, pp. 95-99.

Dismore, James. *5 Kingdom Ways.* Fort Collins, Colorado: Kingdom Ways Companies, 2002.

Donlon, J.P. "CEO of the year," *Chief Executive Magazine,* July 2000.

Drucker, Peter, "Tomorrow's manager," Success, October 1993, *80.*

Dunham, Archie. Personal communication to the authors, at the annual convention of *Fellowship of Companies for Christ International,* Cancun, Mexico, October 2002.

Fenn, Donna. "Made in the USA," *INC. Magazine,* January 2002.

Fitzgerald, Catherine, & Berger, Jennifer Garvey (Eds.). *Executive Coaching: Practices and Perspectives.* Palo Alto, California: Davies-Black Publishing, 2002.

Folk, Jeannie M., Garrison, Ray H., & Noreen, Eric W. *Introduction to Managerial Accounting.* Boston, MA: McGraw-Hill Irwin, 2002.

Friedman, Milton. *Capitalism and Freedom.* Chicago: University of Chicago Press, 1962.

Gerber, Michael E. *The E Myth Revisited: Why Most Small Businesses Don't Work and What to Do About It.* New York: Harper Business, 2001.

Greco, Susan. "The power of balance," The Inc 500 America's Fastest-Growing Private Companies, *INC Magazine,* October 15, 2000.

Greenberg, Jerald, & Baron, Robert A. *Behavior in Organizations: Understanding and Managing the Human Side of Work, Seventh Edition.* Upper Saddle River, New Jersey: Prentice Hall, 2000.

Hall, James A. *Information Systems Auditing and Assurance.* Cincinnati: South-Western College Publishing, 2000.

Hansen, Mark Victor, & Allen, Robert G. *The One Minute Millionaire: The Enlightened Way to Wealth.* New York: Harmony Books, 2002.

Hill, Alexander. *Just Business: Christian Ethics for the Marketplace.* Downers Grove, Illinois: InterVarsity Press, 1997.

Hodgetts, Richard M., & Luthans, Fred. *International Management: Culture, Strategy, and Behavior, Fifth Edition.* Boston: McGraw-Hill Irwin, 2003.

Hofman, Mike. "If at first you don't succeed," *INC. Magazine*, January 2002.

Holt, Laurence, & Neil, Dale. *You Can Start A Business.* Sweden: International Christian Chamber of Commerce, 2002. (Book and video series)

Holy Bible, New International Version. Colorado Springs, Colorado: International Bible Society, 1973, 1978, and 1984.

Hyatt, Joshua. "Transforming experiences," The Inc 500 America's Fastest-Growing Private Companies, *INC Magazine*, October 15, 2000.

Inkpen, Andrew C. "Managing balance in career and life: An interview with champion triathlete Scott Tinley," *Journal of Management Inquiry*, March 2001.

Interlinear NRSV-NIV Parallel New Testament in Greek and English. Alfred Marshall (Ed.). Grand Rapids, Michigan: Zondervan Publishing House of Harper Collins Publishers, 1993.

Jenson, Ron. *Achieving Authentic Success: 10 Timeless Life Principles That Will Maximize Your Real Potential.* San Diego, California: Future Achievement International, 2001.

Joyce, William, Nohria, Nitin, & Roberson, Bruce. *What Really Works: The 4+2 Formula For Sustained Business Success.* New York: HarperBusiness, 2003.

Kant, Immanuel. *Grounding for the Metaphysics of Morals.* Indianapolis: Hackett, 1988, pp. 30-31 (translation modified).

Kant, Immanuel. *Practical Philosophy* (edited by M. J. Gregor). Cambridge: Cambridge University Press, 1996, pp. 611-615.

Kobasa, S. C., Maddi, S. R., & Pucretti, M.C. "Personality and exercise as buffers in the stress-illness relationship," *Journal of Behavioral Medicine*, 1982, *5*:391-404.

Kobasa, S. C., Maddi, S. R., & Kahn, S. "Hardiness and health: A prospective study," *Journal of Personality and Social Psychology*, 1982, *42*:168-177.

Kooser, Amanda. "The next level," *Entrepreneur*, June 2002.

Kotler, Philip. *Kotler on Marketing: How to Create, Win, and Dominate Markets*. New York: The Free Press, 1999.

Kotler, Philip. *Marketing Management, Eleventh Edition*. Upper Saddle River, New Jersey: Prentice Hall, 2003.

Knoblauch, Jörg, & Stängel, Lars. *TEMP Methode—Effektive Unternehmensführung: So machen Sie Ihr Unternehmen fit für die "Bundesliga."* Giengen, Germany: Tempus Seminare, 2000.

Knoblauch, Jörg, Stängel, Lars, Rekers, George A., & Rekers, Steven G. *How to Effectively Manage Your Company to Maximize Performance*. Columbia, South Carolina: University Studies Council, Inc., 2001.

Levy, Michael, & Weitz, Barton A. *Retailing Management, Third Edition*. Boston: McGraw-Hill Irwin, 1998.

Lloyd, Thomas. *Instructor's Manual to Accompany Management: Competing in the New Era, Fifth Edition*. Boston: McGraw-Hill Irwin, 2002.

McGregor, Douglas. *The Human Side of Enterprise*. New York: McGraw-Hill, 1960.

Morse, Gardiner. "Why we misread motives," Motivating People: How to Get the Most from Your Organization, *Harvard Business Review (Special Issue)*, *81*(1), January 2003.

Moyer, R. Charles, McGuigan, James R., & Kretlow, William J. *Contemporary Financial Management.* Mason, Ohio: Thomson South-Western, 2003.

Pande, Peter S., Neuman, Robert P., & Cavanagh, Roland R. *The Six Sigma Way: How GE, Motorola, and Other Top Companies Are Honing Their Performance*. New York: McGraw-Hill, 2000.

Pearson, Andrall E. "Tough-Minded Ways to Get Innovative," The Innovative Enterprise: Turning Ideas into Profit, *Harvard Business Review (Special Issue), 80*(8), August 2002.

Peters, Thomas J., & Waterman Jr., Robert H. *In Search of Excellence: Lessons from America's Best-Run Companies.* New York: Harper & Row, 1982.

Pierce, John A., II, & Robinson, Richard B., Jr. *Strategic Management: Formulation, Implementation, and Control, Eighth Edition.* Boston: McGraw-Hill Irwin, 2003.

Pierce, Jon L., & Newstrom, John W. *The Manager's Bookshelf: A Mosaic of Contemporary Views, Sixth Edition.* Upper Saddle River, New Jersey: Prentice Hall, 2002.

Porter, Michael E. "From competitive advantage to corporate strategy," *Managerial Excellence*, p. 137.

Rae, Scott B., & Wong, Kenman L. *Beyond Integrity: A Judeo-Christian Approach to Business Ethics.* Grand Rapids, Michigan: Zondervan Publishing House of Harper Collins Publishers, 1996.

Rajat, Gupta (Foreward), & Stone Nan (Preface), *Managerial Excellence: McKinsey Award Winners from the Harvard Business Review 1980-1994.* A Harvard Business Review Book, 1996.

Rasiel, Ethan M. *The McKinsey Way: Using the Techniques of the World's Top Strategic Consultants to Help You and Your Business.* New York: McGraw-Hill, 1999.

Rayport, Jeffrey F., & Jaworski, Bernard J. *e-Commerce.* New York: McGraw-Hill/Irwin, 2001.

Ross, W. D. *The Right and the Good.* London: Oxford University Press, 1930.

Shaw, William H., & Barry, Vincent. *Moral Issues in Business, Eighth Edition.* Belmont, CA: Wadsworth Thomas Learning, 2001.

Simons, Tony. "The high cost of lost trust," *Harvard Business Review, 80*(9), September 2002.

Skinner, Von Essen, & Mersham. *Handbook of Public Relations Sixth Edition.* Cape Town, South Africa: Oxford University Press Southern Africa, 2001.

Solomon, Robert C. "It's good business," in William H. Shaw & Vincent Barry, *Moral Issues in Business, Eighth Edition*. Belmont, CA: Wadsworth Thomas Learning, 2001, pp. 35-43.

Torres, Nichole. "Doing good," *Entrepreneur*, June 2002.

Torres, Nichole. "Please don't go: Turnover isn't necessarily a fact of life. Learn to keep your employees in the fold," *Entrepreneur*, November 2002, p. 24.

Tuleja, Tad. *Beyond the Bottom Line*. New York: Penguin Books, 1987.

Walsh, Ciaran. *Key Management Ratios: How to Analyse, Compare and Control the Figures that Drive Company Value*. London, England: Pitman Publishing, 1993.

Webster's Third New International Dictionary of the English Language Unabridged. Chicago: Merriam-Webster/Encyclopedia Britannica, Volume II, 1986, p. 1497.

Weinstein, Art, & Johnson, William C. *Designing and Delivering Superior Customer Value*. Boca Raton: St. Lucie Press, 1999.

Zikmund, William G. *Business Research Methods, Seventh Edition*. Mason, Ohio: Thomson South-Western, 2003.

Notes

PREFACE

[1] Folk, Garrison, & Noreen, 2002, page 2.
[2] Folk, Garrison, & Noreen, 2002, page 2.
[3] Holt, 2002, page 119.

INTRODUCTION

[1] From Zig Ziglar, *See You at the Top*, Pelican Publishing, as quoted by Holt, 2002, page 42.
[2] Bogan & English, 1994, page 16.
[3] Knoblauch & Stängel, 2000.
[4] *Webster's Third New International Dictionary* (Volume III, page 2218).
[5] *Webster's Third New International Dictionary* (Volume I, page 203).
[6] Camp, 1995, page 247.
[7] Bateman & Snell, 2000, page 11-13.
[8] Knoblauch, Stängel, Rekers, & Rekers, 2001.
[9] Pearson, 2002.

PROLOGUE

[1] Camp, 1995, page 27.
[2] Bateman & Snell, 2000, page 490.
[3] Knoblauch, Stängel, Rekers, & Rekers, 2001.
[4] 2 Chronicles 1:7, 10.
[5] Holt, 2002, Introduction, page vii.

DYNAMIC ONE

[1] Porter, page 137.
[2] Kotler, 2003, page 89.
[3] Knoblauch & Stängel, 2000.
[4] Hansen & Allen, 2002, page xiii.
[5] Kotler, 2003, page 92.
[6] Luke 14:28-30.
[7] Proverbs 21:5.

DYNAMIC TWO

[1] Beatty & Burkholder, 1996, page 50.
[2] Holt, 2002, page 115.
[3] Greenberg & Baron, 2000, page 139.
[4] Greenberg & Baron, 2000, pages 140-141.
[5] Zikmund, 2003, page 328.

DYNAMIC THREE

[1] http://www.greenleaf.org/leadership/servant-leadership/What-is-Servant-Leadership.html
[2] Hofman, 2002, page 104.
[3] Bennis & Nanus, 1985, page 27.
[4] Folk, Garrison, & Noreen, 2002, page 20.
[5] Joyce, Nohria, & Roberson, 2003, page 246.
[6] Adapted from Bateman & Snell, 2002, page 380.
[7] Joyce, Nohria, & Roberson, 2003, page 201.
[8] http://www.greenleaf.org/leadership/servant-leadership/What-is-Servant-Leadership.html
[9] Matthew 23:11.
[10] Philippians 2:4.
[11] Collins, 2001, page 27.
[12] Collins, 2001, page 28.
[13] Collins, 2001, page 28.
[14] Bateman & Snell, 2000; Hill, 1997.
[15] Beatty & Burkholder, 1996, page 32.

DYNAMIC FOUR

[1] Proverbs 21:5.
[2] Bateman & Snell, 2002, page 506.
[3] Bateman & Snell, 2002, page 506.
[4] Zikmund, 2003, page 480.

DYNAMIC FIVE

[1] Holt, 2002, page 181.
[2] Shaw & Barry, 2001, pages 25-26.
[3] Leviticus 19:18.
[4] Hill, 1997.
[5] Proverbs 11:3.
[6] Proverbs 11:1.
[7] John 3:19.
[8] Simons, 2002.
[9] Proverbs 13:15.

[10] From Mark Schwartz and Meir Tamari, *A Halakhic Corporate Code of Ethics*, Center for Business Ethics, Vol 3, 4, Jerusalem College of Technology, as quoted by Holt, 2002, page 181.
[11] Beatty & Burkholder, 1996, pages 43-44.
[12] From Gustav von Hertzen, *Cynics and Progress Motors*, Scandinavian Institutes for Administrative Research (SIAR) Dokumentation AB, as quoted by Holt, 2002, page 173.
[13] Jenson, 2001, pages 88-89.

DYNAMIC SIX

[1] Jenson, 2001, page 124.
[2] Greco, 2000, page 106.
[3] Barker, 2000, page 18.
[4] Hyatt, 2000, pages 9-11.
[5] Psalm 127:2.
[6] Greco, 2000, page 110.
[7] Inkpen, 2001, pages 76-81.
[8] Donlon, 2000.
[9] Greco, 2000, page 107.
[10] Beatty & Burkholder, 1996, page 41.

DYNAMIC SEVEN

[1] Rajat & Stone, 1996, page 79.
[2] Bateman & Snell, 2002, page 564.
[3] Bateman & Snell, 2002, page 564.
[4] The authors acknowledge that the major sources of information for this chapter are (a) a tour they took of Drilbox, a Knoblauch Group Company, (b) the TEMP German language business seminar by Jörg Knoblauch, M.B.A., Ph.D. (Knoblauch & Stängel, 2000), (c) Knoblauch, Stängel, Rekers, & Rekers, 2001. Drilbox received the highest award for efficiency from the German government, ranking #1 among all companies in the nation.
[5] *INC Magazine*, The Inc 500 America's Fastest-Growing Private Companies, "Man vs. machine," October 15, 2002, page 79.
[6] "A kanban control system uses a signaling device to regulate just-in-time (JIT) flows. Kanban means 'sign' or 'instuction card' in Japanese. In a paperless control system, containers can be used instead of cards. The cards or containers make up the kanban pull system. The authority to produce or supply additional parts comes from downstream operations" (Chase, Aquilano, & Jacobs, 2001, page 399).

DYNAMIC EIGHT

[1] Jenson, 2001, page 187.

[2] The authors acknowledge that the major sources of information for this chapter are (a) a tour they took of Drilbox, a Knoblauch Group Company, (b) the TEMP German language business seminar by Jörg Knoblauch, M.B.A., Ph.D. (Knoblauch & Stängel, 2000), (c) Knoblauch, Stängel, Rekers, & Rekers, 2001. Drilbox received the highest award for efficiency from the German government, ranking #1 among all companies in the nation.

[3] Joyce, Nohria, & Roberson, 2003, page 49.

[4] Jenson, 2001, page 187.

DYNAMIC NINE

[1] *INC Magazine,* What to Start Now, "Forget market timing," March 2002, page 71.

[2] Folk, Garrison, & Noreen, 2002, page 29.

[3] Folk, Garrison, & Noreen, 2002, page 2.

[4] The authors acknowledge that the major sources of information for this chapter are (a) a tour they took of Drilbox, a Knoblauch Group Company, (b) the TEMP German language business seminar by Jörg Knoblauch, M.B.A., Ph.D. (Knoblauch & Stängel, 2000), (c) Knoblauch, Stängel, Rekers, & Rekers, 2001. Drilbox received the highest award for efficiency from the German government, ranking #1 among all companies in the nation.

[5] Folk, Garrison, & Noreen, 2002, page 3.

[6] Folk, Garrison, & Noreen, 2002, page 4.

[7] Fenn, January 2002, pages 81-82.

DYNAMIC TEN

[1] Fenn, 2002, pages 81-82.

[2] Beatty & Burkholder, 1996, page 60.

[3] The authors acknowledge that the major sources of information for this chapter are (a) a tour they took of Drilbox, a Knoblauch Group Company, (b) the TEMP German language business seminar by Jörg Knoblauch, M.B.A., Ph.D., (Knoblauch, Stängel, Rekers, & Rekers, 2001), (c) Knoblauch & Stängel, 2000. Drilbox received the highest award for efficiency from the German government.

DYNAMIC ELEVEN

[1] Knoblauch & Stängel, 2000.

[2] Zikmund, 2003, page 31.

[3] Knoblauch & Stängel, 2000.

[4] Collins, 2001, page 148.

[5] *INC Magazine,* What to Start Now, "Book smart," March 2002, page 136.

[6] Drucker, 1993.

DYNAMIC TWELVE

[1] Zikmund, 2003, page 574.
[2] Hall, 2000, pages 9-12.
[3] Holt, 2002, page 161.
[4] Proverbs 27:23.

DYNAMIC THIRTEEN

[1] Knoblauch & Stängel, 2000.
[2] Knoblauch & Stängel, 2000.
[3] Knoblauch & Stängel, 2000.
[4] Knoblauch & Stängel, 2000.
[5] Beatty & Burkholder, 1996, page 63.

DYNAMIC FOURTEEN

[1] Beatty & Burkholder, 1996, page 41.
[2] Ephesians 5:8b, 9, 12-14a.
[3] Matthew 7:12.
[4] Bateman & Snell, 2002, page 362.
[5] "Transformational leader: a leader who transforms a vision into reality and motivates people to transcend their personal interests for the good of the group" (Bateman & Snell, 2002, page 397).
[6] Proverbs 12:18-19.
[7] Ephesians 4:25.
[8] Beatty & Burkholder, 1996, page 55.
[9] Zikmund, 2003, page 598.

DYNAMIC FIFTEEN

[1] Jenson, 2001, page 141.
[2] Jenson, 2001, page 31.
[3] Greenberg & Baron 2000, page 129.
[4] Greenberg & Baron 2000, page 130.
[5] Morse, 2003.
[6] Proverbs 14:23a.

DYNAMIC SIXTEEN

[1] Jenson, 2001, page 106.
[2] Proverbs 15:22.
[3] Beatty & Burkholder, 1996, pages 28-29.

DYNAMIC SEVENTEEN

[1] Beatty & Burkholder, 1996, page 49.
[2] Beatty & Burkholder, 1996, page 6.

[3] Pierce & Newstrom, 2002, page 56.
[4] Joyce, Nohria, & Roberson, 2003, page 194.
[5] Joyce, Nohria, & Roberson, 2003, page 193.
[6] Greenberg & Baron, 2000, page 76.
[7] Greenberg & Baron, 2000, pages 78-79.
[8] Pierce & Newstrom, 2002, page 54.
[9] Beatty & Burkholder, 1996, page 52.
[10] Proverbs 19:20.

DYNAMIC EIGHTEEN

[1] Greenberg & Baron, 2000, page 281.
[2] Greenberg & Baron, 2000, page 251.
[3] Greenberg & Baron, 2000, page 252.
[4] Greenberg & Baron, 2000, pages 378-379.
[5] Greenberg & Baron, 2000, pages 379.
[6] Joyce, Nohria, & Roberson, 2003, page 194.
[7] Joyce, Nohria, & Roberson, 2003, pages 194-195.
[8] Joyce, Nohria, & Roberson, 2003, page 195.
[9] Holt, 2002, page 89.

DYNAMIC NINETEEN

[1] Jenson, 2001, page 48.
[2] Collins, 2001, page 51.
[3] Beatty & Burkholder, 1996, page 90.
[4] *INC Magazine*, The Inc 500 America's Fastest-Growing Private Companies, "Employment guaranteed for life," October 15, 2002, pages 74-76.
[5] Beatty & Burkholder, 1996, page 11.

DYNAMIC TWENTY

[1] *Let's Talk Business Network,* website at www.ltbn.com
[2] *Let's Talk Business Network,* website at www.ltbn.com
[3] Jenson, 2001, page 73.
[4] *The Autobiography of Andrew Carnegie* by Andrew Carnegie; *Andrew Carnegie* by Joseph Frazier Wall; *Andrew Carnegie and the Rise of Big Business* by Harold C. Livesay; *Let's Talk Business Network* website: www.ltbn.com
[5] Kobasa, Maddi, & Pucretti, 1982, pages 391-404; Kobasa, Maddi, & Kahn, 1982, pages 168-177.

DYNAMIC TWENTY-ONE

[1] Beatty & Burkholder, 1996, page 66.
[2] Greenberg & Baron, 2000, pages 219-221.

[3] Proverbs 1:5.
[4] Torres, 2002, page 24.

DYNAMIC TWENTY-TWO

[1] Beatty & Burkholder, 1996, page 28.
[2] Beatty & Burkholder, 1996, page 93.
[3] Beatty & Burkholder, 1996, page 28.
[4] Proverbs 9:9.
[5] Jenson 2001, page 143.
[6] Joyce, Nohria, & Roberson, 2003, page 188.
[7] Joyce, Nohria, & Roberson, 2003, pages 190-192.
[8] Pierce & Newstrom, 2002, page 55.
[9] Beatty & Burkholder, 1996, page 93.

DYNAMIC TWENTY-THREE

[1] Jenson, 1996, page 161.
[2] Greenberg & Baron, 2000, pages 178-179.
[3] Proverbs 11: 24.
[4] I Timothy 5:18; Luke 10:7b.
[5] Luke 10:7b.
[6] Proverbs 11:25.
[7] Luke 6:31.
[8] Joyce, Nohria, & Roberson, 2003, page 217.
[9] Joyce, Nohria, & Roberson, 2003, page 218.
[10] Proverbs 17:2.

DYNAMIC TWENTY-FOUR

[1] Beatty & Burkholder, 1996, page 23.
[2] Bateman & Snell, 2002, page 124.
[3] Joyce, Nohria, & Roberson, 2003, page 258.
[4] Bateman & Snell, 2002, pages 344, 348-350.
[5] *INC Magazine*, The Inc 500 America's Fastest-Growing Private Companies, "6 ways to outrun the competition," October 15, 2002, page 58.
[6] Beatty & Burkholder, 1996, page 23.

DYNAMIC TWENTY-FIVE

[1] Zikmund, 2003, page 336.
[2] Beth Whitehouse, "Season's greetings," *Newsday*, December 11, 2000, page B6, as quoted by Kotler, 2003, page 280.
[3] Luke 14:28-30.

[4] Jennifer Porter Gore, "Small business is big at BB&T," *Bank Marketing*, August 1998: 10, as quoted by Kotler, 2003, page 297.
[5] Kotler, 2003, page 22.
[6] *INC Magazine*, The Inc 500 America's Fastest-Growing Private Companies, "6 ways to outrun the competition," October 15, 2002, page 56.
[7] Kotler, 2003, page 24.

DYNAMIC TWENTY-SIX

[1] Joyce, Nohria, & Roberson, 2003, page 119.
[2] Joyce, Nohria, & Roberson, 2003, page 232.
[3] *Harvard Business Review* (Special Issue) "Inspiring innovation," August 2002, *80*(8), page 47.
[4] Beatty & Burkholder, 1996, page 27.
[5] *INC Magazine*, The Inc 500 America's Fastest-Growing Private Companies, "6 ways to outrun the competition," October 15, 2002, page 56.
[6] Beatty & Burkholder, 1996, page 27.

DYNAMIC TWENTY-SEVEN

[1] Beatty & Burkholder, 1996, page 27.
[2] Knoblauch, Stängel, Rekers, & Rekers, 2001.
[3] Folk, Garrison, & Noreen, 2002, page 50.
[4] Fenn, 2002, page 78.
[5] Folk, Garrison, & Noreen 2002, page 50.

DYNAMIC TWENTY-EIGHT

[1] Skinner, Von Essen, and Mersham, Forword by Melvin L Sharp.
[2] Skinner, Von Essen, and Mersham, 2001, page 3.
[3] Skinner, Von Essen, and Mersham, 2001, page 3.
[4] Skinner, Von Essen, and Mersham, 2001, page 4.
[5] Skinner, Von Essen, and Mersham, 2001, page 4.
[6] Torres, 2002, page 132.
[7] Proverbs 22:1.

DYNAMIC TWENTY-NINE

[1] Beatty & Burkholder, 1996, page 27 (in a 1993 letter to the shareholders).
[2] Gerber, 2001, pages 189-192.
[3] Kooser, 2002, page 64.
[4] Jenson, 2001, page 40.

DYNAMIC THIRTY

[1] Kotler, 2003, page 637.
[2] Kotler, 2003, page 637.
[3] Kotler, 2003, page 23.

DYNAMIC THIRTY-ONE

[1] From Charles Handy, *The Empty Raincoat*, London: Arrow Business Books, 1995, as quoted by Holt, 2002, page 72.
[2] Philippians 2:4.
[3] *INC Magazine*, The Inc 500 America's Fastest-Growing Private Companies, "6 ways to outrun the competition," October 15, 2002, page 58.

DYNAMIC THIRTY-THREE

[1] Beatty & Burkholder, 1996, page 27.
[2] *INC Magazine*, The Inc 500 America's Fastest-Growing Private Companies, "6 ways to outrun the competition," October 15, 2002, page 56.
[3] Luke 10:27b.
[4] Luke 10:29b.
[5] Luke 10:30-36.
[6] Luke 10:37b.
[7] Beatty & Burkholder, 1996, page 27.

EPILOGUE

[1] Beatty & Burkholder, 1996, page 12.

INDEX

About the Authors

Matthew G. Rekers, M.B.A., is the President and CEO of 33Dynamics LLC, and the President and CEO of 33Dynamics Consulting LLC. He previously served as the President and COO of Rekers and Company LLC, and as the Vice President for Program Development for InterAct International, Inc. Mr. Rekers earned his Bachelors of Science degree in Business Administration, cum laude, from the University of South Carolina with a major in accounting, and his Master of Business Administration degree from Winthrop University. He is the co-author of the 33Dynamics™ Seminar and Consulting System that includes 33 Participant Workbooks and the associated set of 33 curriculum books for executive seminar leaders. He is a business consultant for 33Dynamics Consulting LLC, and a seminar leader for *There's Room at the Top Executive Development Seminars* offered by 33Dynamics LLC. He can be contacted at <matt@33dynamics.com>.

George A. Rekers, Ph.D., M.B.A., is a tenured professor at the University of South Carolina, and the Chairman and CEO of InterAct International, Inc. Dr. Rekers has 22 years of executive experience in leading four small-sized corporations as President or CEO, and has served on seven corporate boards. As a Visiting Scholar and Research Fellow at Harvard University, Dr. Rekers was mentored by Professor David McClelland who is internationally known for his practical studies of executive and employee motivation. Professor Rekers has presented hundreds of seminars, workshops, and invited lectures in dozens of countries in Africa, Asia, Europe, Latin America, North America, and the Middle East. He focused on executive management in his M.B.A. program, received his Ph.D. in human developmental psychology from the University of California, Los Angeles, and earned his Th.D. in practical theology from the University of South Africa. Dr. Rekers is designated as a Certified Seminar Leader by the American Seminar Leaders Association. He is the co-author of the 33Dynamics™ Seminar and Consulting System, and the author or editor of ten books and over 100 academic publications in applied psychology. He is an executive consultant for 33Dynamics Consulting LLC, and a seminar leader for *There's Room at the Top Executive Seminars* offered by 33Dynamics LLC. He can be contacted at <george@33dynamics.com>.